STORIES FROM THE
MAHĀBHĀRATA

PART THREE

A SANSKRIT LANGUAGE COURSE

Seven Sanskrit Coursebooks for Beginners

Pages: viii, 76   Pages: viii, 76   Pages: viii, 60

Pages: xiv, 162   Pages: xv, 189   Pages: xviii, 125   Pages: xiv, 137

All books are A4 Size (297x210 mm) and available in paperback, spiral bound and hardbound.

Extracts from reviews:

The textbooks are reader friendly and enhance the user's creative skills by providing the opportunity to draw and paint along with stories.

—THE SPEAKING TREE,
February 26, 2012

I'm simply overwhelmed with joy just looking at these seven coursebooks. ..... Even after following a traditional twelve-year grammar course, the curiosity of Sanskrit lovers is not satiated. ... For such people this *Bhagiratha* (great) attempt is certainly praiseworthy.

—PROF. DAYANANDA BHARGAVA
March 26th, 2012

It is a privilege for me be invited to introduce this set of text books... Only a few students are likely to have the opportunity to go on to study Sanskrit in depth, so that they can enjoy reading Sanskrit by themselves. ..... And the few who go further will be grateful that these books have launched them on an unforgettable experience.

—PROF. RICHARD GOMBRICH
in his 'Preface'

These coursebooks are well-graded, and supported by appropriate illustrations that make them very attractive to learners, particularly the young. Today many Indian and foreign schools/colleges offer Sanskrit as an optional subject. For such students these books are a very effective means of introducing Sanskrit, which they might not have studied previously. These books could also be useful for those involved in performing arts, such as dance and music, or for students of Yoga and Ayurveda—subjects which have many Sanskrit references.

—PROF. SATYAVRAT SHASTRI
in his 'Foreword'

Stories From

The Mahābhārata

A Sanskrit Coursebook for Intermediate Level

Edited by

WARWICK JESSUP

ELENA JESSUP

PART III

MOTILAL BANARSIDASS PUBLISHERS
PRIVATE LIMITED • DELHI

First Edition : Delhi, **2016**

Published under arrangements with
St James Schools,
Sanskrit Department, London

ISBN : 978-81-208-4014-0 (PB Part I)
ISBN : 978-81-208-4015-7 (PB Part II)
ISBN : 978-81-208-4016-4 (PB Part III)
ISBN : 978-81-208-4013-3 (Set HB)

MOTILAL BANARSIDASS

41 U.A. Bungalow Road, Jawahar Nagar, Delhi 110 007
8 Mahalaxmi Chamber, 22 Bhulabhai Desai Road, Mumbai 400 026
203 Royapettah High Road, Mylapore, Chennai 600 004
236, 9th Main III Block, Jayanagar, Bengaluru 560 011
Sanas Plaza, 1302 Baji Rao Road, Pune 411 002
8 Camac Street, Kolkata 700 017
Ashok Rajpath, Patna 800 004
Chowk, Varanasi 221 001

The Sanskritpada™, SCcomp™ and Flags2 Sanskrit fonts used in this book are designed and
distributed by David Hockley, Oxford (tel. 01844 339944).   © 2003 David Hockley.

COVER DRAWING: Abhimanyu breaks into the Wheel Formation

Printed in India
by RP Jain at NAB Printing Unit,
A-44, Naraina Industrial Area, Phase I, New Delhi–110028
and published by JP Jain for Motilal Banarsidass Publishers (P) Ltd,
41 U.A. Bungalow Road, Jawahar Nagar, Delhi-110007

The Editors wish to acknowledge the role played by Annette Morgan and other members of the St James Sanskrit faculty in the preparation of the material for this Sanskrit course, and would also like to thank Mariano de la Torre for the illustrations and Michael Croza-Ross for his unstinting work in designing these volumes.

CONTENTS

Teaching Sanskrit

INTRODUCTION

The Sanskrit language in many parts of the world is a new element in today's education. It is an ideal study for the young because its systematic grammar orders the student's mind. At the same time, Sanskrit literature provides the student with an exciting and profound interaction with a classical culture. Furthermore, because Sanskrit is very close to the source of all Indo-European languages, it helps the student appreciate the underlying structure of language as a whole.

'Stories from the Mahābhārata', a new series of Sanskrit textbooks, presents the epic *'Mahābhārata'* in stories which develop the students' knowledge of grammar in a gradual way. It is strongly suggested that students should have completed Parts One and Two and also the preceding section of this course, *'The Story of Rāma' (Parts 1 and 2)*, before starting this book.

READING AND WRITING THE *DEVANĀGARĪ* SCRIPT

Fluent reading and writing of the *devanāgarī* script is essential at this point. If the students are commencing this book after the holidays, you will probably want to spend some time practising reading, writing and dictation exercises.

ORAL AND LISTENING EXERCISES

When teaching this course, it is very useful to have an oral component to each lesson. If students spend all their time doing written work and never speaking the language, their learning will not stick. Similarly, listening exercises (i.e., listening to a story read in Sanskrit and then answering questions about it) help to immerse the student in the 'Sanskrit mindset'. Thus, the exercises given in this book can always be used as oral and listening exercises, and games and competitions are even more effective.

The same is true in learning paradigms. Students should not expect that they will learn their case endings by looking them up. Learning of paradigms should be primarily through recitation in the traditional manner (i.e., by the order of singular, dual and plural for each case). As a supporting method, learning for tests may also be done by looking for patterns of recurring words and similarities with other paradigms. Regular oral and written testing of paradigms is necessary to ensure that they are known accurately and by heart. This applies particularly to the paradigms previously learnt.

Not all the exercises in this book need to be completed: some are optional and should be used according to the teacher's discrimination. It is essential that there be a forward momentum to this study. Some exercises, especially *sandhi* exercises, can be filled in by the students in this book.

VOCABULARY

The approach to vocabulary in these books is different from that presented in the earlier textbooks. All new words in a story are underlined, and their English equivalents will be found at the bottom of the page on which they are working. However, in each chapter there is a list of new vocabulary words. These should be learned and tested, and could usefully form a component of any end-of-term exam.

Verbs are given a different treatment to that of the earlier course. New verbs are presented in three forms, namely the *dhātu,* the First Person singular (i.e., the –ति form) and the indeclinable participle (i.e., the –त्वा form).

In this third part of the series, the vocabulary for IGCSE Sanskrit is gradually introduced. Asterisked words need to be known in both Sanskrit to English and vice versa. Words without asterisks need to be known only from Sanskrit to English.

Each chapter includes a story. It would be helpful to give a written or oral test on the new vocabulary before starting the story.

NOTES TO TEACHERS

Advice to the teacher is indicated in italics.

The Sanskrit Alphabet and its Pronunciation

अ	a	*as in*	approach		ढ	ḍha	*as in*	godhood*
आ	ā	*as in*	star		ण	ṇa	*as in*	under*
इ	i	*as in*	if		त	ta	*as in*	table
ई	ī	*as in*	feel		थ	tha	*as in*	anthill
उ	u	*as in*	book		द	da	*as in*	day
ऊ	ū	*as in*	food		ध	dha	*as in*	godhead
ऋ	ṛ		A sound made with the tip of the tongue raised but not quite touching the roof of the mouth (something like the ri in 'ring').		न	na	*as in*	no
					प	pa	*as in*	pure
ए	e	*as in*	say		फ	pha	*as in*	loop-hole
ऐ	ai	*as in*	my		ब	ba	*as in*	baby
ओ	o	*as in*	home		भ	bha	*as in*	abhor
औ	au	*as in*	now		म	ma	*as in*	mother
क	ka	*as in*	kite		य	ya	*as in*	yellow
ख	kha	*as in*	block-head		र	ra	*as in*	rosy*
ग	ga	*as in*	gate		ल	la	*as in*	lady
च	gha	*as in*	log-hut		व	va	*as in*	awake
ङ	ṅa	*as in*	long		श	śa	*as in*	shall
च	ca	*as in*	chalk		ष	ṣa	*as in*	show*
छ	cha	*as in*	catch him		स	sa	*as in*	slug
ज	ja	*as in*	jug		ह	ha	*as in*	heaven
झ	jha	*as in*	hedgehog					
ञ	ña	*as in*	cringe		ं	ṃ		*as in a pure nasal*
ट	ṭa	*as in*	take*		ः	ḥ		*as in an exhaled breath*
ठ	ṭha	*as in*	anthill*					
ड	ḍa	*as in*	do*					

* with the tongue raised to the roof of the mouth

Note to Teachers

In addition to their revision of the grammatical terms described on pages 2–4, students should briefly review, and be tested on, the forms of the following words:

NOUNS	VERBS	PRONOUNS
रामः	भवति	तत्, सः, सा
मित्रम्	भविष्यति	किम्, कः, का
सीता	अभवत्	अहम्
नदी	वर्धते	त्वम्
हरिः	वर्धिष्यते	
गुरुः	अवर्धत	
धातृ	अस्ति	
मातृ	आसीत्	
पितृ	खाद्यते	
राजन्	करोति	
कर्मन्	करिष्यति	
मनस्	अकरोत्	
ज्ञानिन्		
ज्ञानिनी		
धीमत्		
धीमती		
मतिः		

Grammatical Terms

NOUN	A **noun** is a person, place or thing.
	e.g. रामः Rāma
	अयोध्या Ayodhyā
	सूत्रम् rope
ADJECTIVE	An **adjective** is a word that describes a noun.
	e.g. पीत॰ yellow
	पाण्डु॰ pale
	The ॰ symbol at the end of these words indicates that they may take endings in three genders, eight cases, and three numbers.
VERB	A **verb** is an action word.
	e.g. पिबति he drinks
	गमिष्यामि I shall go
CASE ENDINGS	The **case ending** of a noun shows the role of that noun in the sentence.
	e.g. रामस्य <u>of</u> Rāma
	सीतया <u>by</u> Sītā
	There are seven cases in Sanskrit plus the vocative:

FIRST CASE ENDING	*often the doer*
VOCATIVE	*the person addressed*
SECOND CASE ENDING	*the object 'done to'*
THIRD CASE ENDING	*by or with*
FOURTH CASE ENDING	*for*
FIFTH CASE ENDING	*from*
SIXTH CASE ENDING	*of*
SEVENTH CASE ENDING	*in (or on)*

AGREEMENT	**Agreement** means that adjectives agree in case, number and gender with the nouns they go with.
	
	e.g. चोरः राक्षसः horrible demon
	         चोराय राक्षसाय for the horrible demon
	         चोरैः राक्षसैः by horrible demons

NUMBER	The **number** of a word shows whether that word is singular, dual or plural.
	
	e.g. खगः bird *(singular)*
	         खगौ two birds *(dual)*
	         खगाः birds *(plural)*
	
	Note that the plural for 'bird' is simply translated as 'birds', while the dual is translated as 'two birds'.

MASCULINE	A **masculine** word names something considered to be male.
	
	e.g. रामः Rāma
	         हरिः Lord
	         गुरुः teacher

FEMININE	A **feminine** word names something considered to be female.
	
	e.g. सीता Sītā
	         नदी river
	         मतिः thought

NEUTER	A **neuter** word names something considered to be neither male nor female. e.g. मित्रम् friend

3

TENSE	The **tense** of a verb shows the time in which the action is happening.

e.g.

खादति	he eats *(present tense)*
खादिष्यति	he will eat *(future tense)*
अखादत्	he ate *(past tense)*

PARADIGM

A **paradigm** (pronounced *par-a-dime*) is a list or table of all the possible forms that a noun, adjective, pronoun or verb can take.

PERSON

A verb can be expressed in one of three Persons. In Sanskrit grammar these are known as:

	SINGULAR	DUAL	PLURAL
First Person	he/she/it	they two	they
Middle Person	you	you two	you
Best Person	I	we two	we

Later languages (for example, Latin and French) deal with these Persons in the opposite order:

	SINGULAR	DUAL	PLURAL
First Person	I	we two	we
Second Person	you	you two	you
Third Person	he/she/it	they two	they

In this course, we shall use the Sanskrit system.

CHAPTER SEVENTEEN

17.1 Epic Civilisation: The Universal Powers (1)

In the Sanskrit epics there is a hierarchy of beings. The देव s, or gods, are the powers in the universe. इन्द्र is considered as the head or chief of the lower देव s. In the Mahābhārata story इन्द्र is the father of Arjuna, while धर्म ('Duty') is the father of Yudhiṣṭhira, and वायु ('Air') is the father of Bhīma.

Arjuna, Yudhiṣṭhira and Bhīma

17.2 IGCSE Vocabulary 1 — Animals

From this point in the course, vocabulary for IGCSE Sanskrit is being introduced gradually in special 'IGCSE Vocabulary' tables, beginning with this one.

अश्वः (m)	horse
ऋषभः (m)	bull
कपिः (m)	monkey
काकः (m)	crow
कुक्कुरः (m)	dog
खगः (m)	bird
गजः (m)	elephant
गर्दभः (m)	donkey
गृध्रः (m)	vulture
बिडालः (m)	cat
मत्स्यः (m)	fish
मूषिकः (m)	mouse
मृगः (m)	forest animal, deer
व्याघ्रः (m)	tiger
शशकः (m)	rabbit
सर्पः (m)	snake
सिंहः (m)	lion

EXERCISE 131

SANSKRIT ZOO QUIZ

The pictures below feature all the animals in the vocabulary at 17.2. From memory, label each of the animals with its Sanskrit name using Sanskrit script.

17.3 Revision of *Visarga Sandhi*

We shall now revise the 'खर्', 'ो', 'Disappearing' and 'र' processes of *visarga sandhi*.

The खर् process has 1 rule and 3 exceptions.

The code खर् = 13 hard (unvoiced) consonants. These are:

क ख च छ ट ठ त थ प फ श ष स

The Rule says:
: before खर् > : खर् (no change)

For example:

खगः पतति > खगः पतति

THE THREE EXCEPTIONS TO THE खर् RULE

These affect words beginning with च छ or त.

Thus:

: before च > श्च
: before छ > श्छ
: before त > स्त

For example:

नरः चरति	>	नरश्चरति
नरः छाया	>	नरश्छाया
नरः तथा	>	नरस्तथा

The ो process has 2 rules.

The code हश् = the 20 soft consonants. These are:

ग च ङ ह ज झ अ य ड ढ ण र
द ध न ल ब भ म व

For this process a विसर्ग after an अ changes to an

ओ sound written as ो.

The first ो Rule says:

अः before हश् > ो हश् (not joined)

For example:

रामः हसति > रामो् हसति

The second ो Rule says:

अः before अ > ोऽ (no space follows)

For example:

रामः अपि > रामोऽपि

Note: The ऽ symbol is called an 'avagraha' and always represents a short अ — it is never sounded!

The 'Disappearing' process has 3 rules.

(**V** = vowels; हश् = soft consonants; **C** = any consonant)

For this process the विसर्ग simply disappears!

The first Rule says:

अः before **V** *(except अ)* > अ **V** (not joined)

For example:

रामः इच्छति > राम इच्छति

The second Rule says:

आः before **V** or हश् > आ **V** or हश् (not joined)

For example:

रामाः अभवन् > रामा अभवन्

रामाः भवन्ति > रामा भवन्ति

The third Rule says:

सः or एषः before **C** > स/एष **C** (not joined)

For example:

सः भवति > स भवति

The र् process has 1 rule.

(**V** = vowel; हश् = soft consonants;
इच् = any vowel except *short or long* अ)

For this process the विसर्ग changes to a र्.

The Rule says:
इच् + : before **V** or हश् > इच् + र् joined to **V** or हश्

For example:

हरिः इति > हरिरिति

गुरुः भवति > गुरुर्भवति

EXERCISE 132

Translate the following simple story, which uses *visarga sandhi*. The word *mṛga* can mean 'forest animal' as well as 'deer'.

1. वने बहवो मृगा अवसन् ।

2. सिंहः सर्वेषाम् मृगाणाम् नृपोऽभवत् ।

3. एकदा सर्पः कपिर्गृध्रश्च सिंहम् आगच्छन् ।

4. वयम् भीताः ।

5. कश्चित् अतीव प्रबलो मृगो वनम् नगरात् उपगच्छति इति अक्रोशन् ।

6. तत् श्रुत्वा सिंहोऽचिन्तयत् ।

7. अहो ।   स न मृगः ।   स नरः ।

8. स शैरस्मान् व्यापादयिष्यति इति ।

9. तदा सिंहः सर्वान् मूषिकान् समागच्छत् अवदत् च . . .

12

EXERCISE 133

Using Sanskrit script, write a sequel in Sanskrit to the above story, using the words for animals from the IGCSE Vocabulary (1) list in section 17.2. The picture below could give you an idea for the sequel. The word for 'net' is *'jālam'*.

A deer, caught in a net, is freed by a mouse.

17.4 *Hal Sandhi* — the Joining of Consonants

A word ending in a **consonant** before a word beginning with a **consonant** or a **vowel** causes *hal sandhi*.

For *hal sandhi* there are only <u>three consonants</u> that are commonly found at the end of words. These three consonants are:

त् — **two rules (eight exceptions)**

म् — **one rule (two parts)**

न् — **six rules** *[see Chapter 18]*

14

17.5 *Hal Sandhi* Rules for त्

There are two *hal sandhi* rules for words ending in त्.

Hal Sandhi for त् Rule 1 + three exceptions

(The code खर् = 13 hard consonants)

This first Rule says:

त् before खर् = No change but the two words join.

For example:

रामात् पतति > रामात्पतति

The exceptions to Rule 1 relate to three hard consonants
च् छ् and श् (of the same family) as follows:

त् before च = च्च
त् before छ = च्छ
त् before श = च्छ

For example:

तत् चरति > तच्चरति
तत् छाया > तच्छाया
तत् शरः > तच्छरः

[See Exercise 134]

EXERCISE 134

Write the correct sandhi for each of the following pairs of words in the light of Rule 1 (and its three exceptions) given on the immediately preceding page.

1. तत् तदा ....

2. अभवत् पतति ....

3. यस्मात् फलम् ....

4. एतत् कदा ....

5. रामात् खगः ....

6. धीमत् पिता ....

7. तस्मात् शान्तिः ....

8. मत् चिबुकम् ....

9. अस्मत् छाया ....

10. तत् सीता ....

11. नरात् चरति ....

12. मत् शिवः ....

Hal Sandhi for त् Rule 2 (in 2 parts + 5 exceptions)

(**V** = vowels; हश् = soft consonants)

The two parts of this second Rule say:

2a. त् before **V** = द् joined to **V**

2b. त् before हश् = द् joined to हश्

For example:

रामात् आसीत् > रामादासीत्

रामात् भवति > रामाद्भवति

[See Exercise 135]

The 5 exceptions to Rule 2 relate to these soft consonants:

ज न म ल ह as follows:

(i) त् before ज = ज्ज

(ii) त् before न = न्न

(iii) त् before म = न्म

(iv) त् before ल = ल्ल

(v) त् before ह = द्ध

[See Exercises 136 and 137]

EXERCISE 135

Write the correct sandhi for each of the following pairs of words in the light of Rule 2 (both parts) as given on the immediately preceding page. Note the special forms when द् is joined to these particular soft consonants:

द् + य > द्य   द् + ध > द्ध   द् + व > द्व

द् + ब > द्ब   द् + र > द्र   द् + ग > द्ग

द् + भ > द्भ   द् + द > द्द

---

1. तत् वा ....

2. तत् इव ....

3. अभवत् गजा ....

4. तत् वचनम् ....

5. तत् तत् ....

6. एतत् गजः ....

7. अस्मत् आसीत् ....

8. वृक्षात् भूमिः ....

9. अपतत् यदा ....

10. रामात् खगः ....

11. युष्मत् धनम् ....

12. तस्मात् ऋषिः ....

13. मत् अस्ति ....

14. रामात् बालिकाः ....

18

EXERCISE 136

Write the correct sandhi for each of the following pairs of words in the light of the ज, न, म, ल and ह exceptions to Rule 2 . Note:

> त् + ज > ज्ज   त् + न > न्न   त् + म > न्म
> त् + ल > ल्ल   त् + ह > द्ध

1. तत् नमति   ....

2. अभवत् मित्रम्   ....

3. अस्मत् जलम्   ....

4. तत् लिखति   ....

5. नृपात् हसति   ....

6. तस्मात् मम   ....

7. तत् लीला   ....

8. युष्मत् हस्तः   ....

9. रामात् न   ....

EXERCISE 137

Write the correct sandhi for each of the following pairs of words observing Rules 1 and 2 for words ending in a final -त् before a word beginning with a खर् or an अच् or a हश्.

1. तत् शिव ....
2. मत् लोकः ....
3. आसीत् अस्ति ....
4. त्वत् लिखति ....
5. अन्यत् तत् ....
6. यत् राक्षसः ....
7. रामात् मित्रम् ....
8. अचलात् हि ....
9. मत् दानम् ....
10. तस्मात् धनम् ....

11. मत् हरिः ....
12. तत् नाम ....
13. अस्मत् च ....
14. अभवत् जितः ....
15. अभवत् च ....
16. आसीत् नृपः ....
17. तत् पतति ....
18. मत् आसीत् ....
19. तत् शान्तिः ....
20. वृक्षात् उल्का ....

17.6 *Hal Sandhi* for Words Ending in -म्

For words ending in म् there is one *hal sandhi* rule comprising the following two parts:

(C = any consonant;   V = a vowel)

(1) म्   before   **C**   =   ˙ **C** (unjoined)

e.g.   रामम् पश्यति   >   रामं पश्यति

(2) म्   before   **V**   =   म् joined to **V**

e.g.   तम् इति   >   तमिति

The nasal sound called 'anusvāra' is represented by a dot (˙) above a letter.

EXERCISE 138

Write the correct *sandhi* for each of the following pairs of words. Remember that the म् only becomes an *anusvāra* when it is followed by a consonant. When it is followed by a vowel it remains and joins up with the vowel.

1. रामम् क्रिया   ....

2. रामम् च   ....

3. माम् दानम्   ....

4. सीताम् शान्तिः   ....

5. हरिम् सः   ....

6. गुरुम् एतद्   ....

7. अग्निम् इति   ....

8. अभवम् उत्तमः   ....

9. रामम् पतन्ति   ....

10. त्वाम् हसति   ....

EXERCISE 139

Write the correct *hal sandhi* for each of the following pairs of words:

1. तत् कुक्कुरः ....
2. वनात् न ....
3. तत् लिखति ....
4. रामम् तत् ....
5. तत् हरिः ....
6. मत् तारका ....
7. अग्निम् च ....
8. वनात् दुःखम् ....
9. मत् शिला ....
10. तत् देवः ....

11. तत् चित्तम् ....
12. अस्मत् एव ....
13. राजवत् जलम् ....
14. गुरुम् एव ....
15. तस्मात् हरितम् ....
16. तत् शिला ....
17. महत् भोजनम् ....
18. एतत् शान्तम् ....
19. अल्पम् शिलम् ....
20. तस्मात् मधु ....

EXERCISE 140

Write the correct *viyoga* forms for each of the following pairs of words given here in *hal sandhi:*

1. रामाद्यदि   ....

2. अभवदेतत्   ....

3. गुरुं च   ....

4. तद्धरिः   ....

5. रामाद्द्रवति   ....

6. मज्जलम्   ....

7. अपतद्यदा   ....

8. तस्माच्छम्भुः   ....

9. अस्मल्लीला   ....

10. तज्जलम्   ....

17.7 Vocabulary for Story 17

*Note to teacher: Words with an asterisk (*) are part of the IGCSE vocabulary.*

NOUNS

* नृपः (m)	king	* वचनम् (n)	statement
* गृध्रः (m)	vulture	* अन्तः (m)	end

ADJECTIVES

* प्राज्ञ°	wise	* श्रेष्ठ°	best
* छिन्न°	cut	* संतुष्ट°	contented

INDECLINABLES

* एकदा	once	* एवम्	thus
* पुनः	again		

DHĀTUS

प्रति + वद् in replying

रक्ष् in protecting

दा in giving

VERBS

* प्रतिवदति   he replies

* रक्षति   he protects

* ददाति   he gives

'-त्वा' ENDINGS

प्रत्युद्य[1]   having replied

रक्षित्वा   having protected

दत्वा   having given

[1]*Notice the* -य *ending instead of* -त्वा.

17.8   Story 17

> # VULTURE TESTS KING ŚIBI'S VIRTUE
>
> A pigeon, hunted by a vulture, asks for King Śibi's protection. The king grants this, but the vulture insists on having instead some of Śibi's own flesh in order to guarantee the pigeon's safety. Śibi gives him some of his flesh but the vulture asks for more. Śibi gives generously, and thereby saves the pigeon. The vulture praises Śibi.

1. शिबिर्नृप आसीत्।

2. एकदा कपोतस्तमागच्छत्।

3. हे प्राज्ञ नृप गृध्रो मां खादिष्यति इति कपोतोऽवदत्।

4. शिबिः प्रत्यवददहं त्वां रक्षिष्यामि इति।

5. गृध्रस्तु नृपस्य वचनं श्रुत्वा अवदद्धे नृप यस्मात्त्वं कपोतं

   मह्यं न ददासि तस्मात्तव मांसं देहि इति।

[continues on p.27]

कपोतः (m)	pigeon	मांसम् (n)	meat, flesh
यस्मात्	since	देहि	give! (*sing. imperative*)

King Śibi sacrifices his own flesh to save a pigeon.

[continued from p.25]

6. शिबिः <u>स्वदेहान्मांसं</u> <u>छित्वा</u> तद्गृध्राय अददात्।

7. गृध्रस्तु संतुष्टो न आसीत्।

8. नृपेण <u>स्वदेहान्मांसं</u> पुनश्छिन्नम्।

9. अन्ते गृध्रः संतुष्टोऽभवत्।

10. एवं <u>कपोतो</u> रक्षितः।

11. गृध्रोऽवदत्त्वं श्रेष्ठो नृपो <u>लोके</u> इति॥

स्वदेहः (m)	own body	छित्वा (m)	having cut
लोकः (m)	world		

EXERCISE 141

Having read through the preceding story carefully, do not write out a translation, but answer in English the following questions. Give Sanskrit names in transliteration.

1. What did the pigeon say to Śibi? (sentence 3)

2. How did Śibi reply? (sentence 4)

3. What did the vulture ask Śibi to give him for food to replace the pigeon? (sentence 5)

4. Translate 'gṛdhraḥ tu saṃtuṣṭaḥ na āsīt'. (sentence 7)

5. How did the vulture describe Śibi in the end? (sentence 11)

CHAPTER EIGHTEEN

18.1 Epic Civilisation: The Universal Powers (2)

The principal powers of the universe are often considered as a trinity. Each god symbolises the unmoving energy, or holder of the power, and each goddess symbolises the moving energy, or the power itself. Thus:

<u>Gods</u>			<u>Goddesses</u>		
Brahmā	—	*the creator*	Sarasvatī	—	*knowledge*
Viṣṇu	—	*the sustainer*	Lakṣmī	—	*wealth*
Śiva	—	*the dissolver*	Pārvatī	—	*law*

Sarasvatī, Lakṣmī and Pārvatī

18.2 The *Hal Sandhi* Rule for -न्

For words ending in न् there is one *hal sandhi* rule comprising the following six parts:

(1) न् before च = ँश्च

e.g. रामान् चरन्ति > रामांश्चरन्ति

(2) न् before त = ँस्त

e.g. रामान् तरन्ति > रामांस्तरन्ति

(3) न् before ज = ञ्ज

e.g. रामान् जलम् > रामाञ्जलम्

(4) न् before श = ञ्श

e.g. रामान् शान्तिः > रामाञ्श्शान्तिः

(5) न् before ल = ँल्ल

e.g. रामान् लभन्ते > रामाँल्लभन्ते

(6) अन् or इन् before V
= अन्न् or इन्न् joined to V

e.g. अभवन् इति > अभवन्निति
(abhavan iti)   (abhavanniti)

तस्मिन् अथ > तस्मिन्नथ
(tasmin atha)   (tasminnatha)

30

EXERCISE 142

Write the correct *hal sandhi* for each of the following pairs of words:

1. तान् तान् ....
2. यस्मिन् इति ....
3. अभवन् आसीत् ....
4. सर्वान् अभवन् ....
5. रामान् च ....
6. अभवन् जिताः ....
7. हरीन् शान्तिः ....
8. यान् लीलाः ....
9. गुरून् तदा ....
10. तस्मिन् एव ....
11. धातॄन् चरन्ति ....
12. रामान् तरन्ति ....

13. तान् भवन्ति ....
14. हस्तान् खादन्ति ....
15. अलिखन् अस्ति ....
16. तान् लोपः ....
17. तस्मिन् कपिः ....
18. अतुदन् इन्द्रः ....
19. तान् एव ....
20. रामान् लोकः ....

18.3 Revision of Verb Types

Apart from the three tenses of present, past and future of an active verb, so far we have also learnt five types of verb forms — those of the passive verb, past passive participles, words ending in *-tavat*, words ending in *-tvā* or *-ya,* and the imperative.

EXERCISE 143

Say what type of verb fits each of the words below. Then translate each word.

	TYPE	TRANSLATION
1. गतः	....	....
2. गतवान्	....	....
3. गच्छतु	....	....
4. खादिताः	....	....
5. खादितवती	....	....
6. खादन्तु	....	....
7. दृश्यते	....	....
8. भव	....	....
9. दृष्टवन्तः	....	....
10. गम्यते	....	....
11. अगम्यत	....	....
12. खाद्यन्ते	....	....
13. भूतम्	....	....
14. भूतवान्	....	....
15. भवत	....	....
16. गच्छ	....	....
17. आगम्य	....	....
18. प्रतिगम्य	....	....
19. गत्वा	....	....
20. अनुभूतम्	....	....

32

18.4 Vocabulary for Story 18

Note to teacher: Words with an asterisk (*) are part of the IGCSE vocabulary.

NOUNS

*राजगृहम् (n)	palace	*सुहृत् (m)		friend, sweetheart
*भयम् (n)	fear	*शाला (f)		room, hall
*सेवकः (m)	servant, attendant	*रात्रिः (f)		night
*राजन् (m) king; *राज्ञी (f) queen		*युद्धम् (n) + करोति		does battle
*भार्या (f)	wife	*देहः (m)		body
*रूपम् (n)	form	*सैनिकः (m)		soldier

ADJECTIVES

*बलिष्ठ॰	strongest, mightiest	*भीत॰	afraid
*सर्व॰	all (*like* तत् *except n. sing.*)		

DHĀTUS

स्निह्	in falling in love with
मिल्	in meeting with
धाव्	in running
नश्	in destroying

VERBS

*स्निह्यति	falls in love with (+ 7th)
*मिलति	he meets with (+ 3rd)
*धावति	he runs
*नाशयति	he destroys

'-त्वा' ENDINGS

स्निग्ध्वा	having fallen in love with (+ 7th)
मिलित्वा	having met with
धावित्वा	having run
नाशयित्वा	having destroyed

18.5 Story 18

KĪCAKA FAILS TO WOO DRAUPADĪ

The Pāṇḍavas, having lost the dice game, are required to live for a year in disguise. They go to the court of King Virāṭa and pretend to be servants of the king. Draupadī takes on the role of servant of the queen. Virāṭa's general, Kīcaka, takes a fancy to Draupadī. She is afraid and tells Bhīma, who is working as chief chef in Virāṭa's kitchen, about Kīcaka's desire for her. Kīcaka tells Draupadī to meet him in the dance-hall at midnight. Instead, Bhīma goes there and kills Kīcaka.

1. पाण्डवा द्रौपदी च राज्ञो विराटस्य राजगृहमगच्छन् ।

2. ते सर्वे कौरवानां भयाद्विराटस्य सेवकानां रूपं कृतवन्तः ।

3. द्रौपदी राज्ञ्याः सेवका अभवत् ।

4. राज्ञो विराटस्य बलिष्ठः सैनिकः कीचको नाम ।

5. कीचको द्रौपद्यामस्निह्यत् ।

[continues on page 36]

रूपम् करोति   takes on a disguise

34

Bhīma kills Kīcaka.

[continued from p.34]

6. मम भार्या भव इति कीचको द्रौपदीमुक्तवान्।

7. भीता द्रौपदी हे सुहृन्नाटकानां शालायां रात्र्यां मिलिष्याव

इति तमुक्तवती।

8. द्रौपदी भीममधावत्तं सर्वमवदच्च।

9. रात्र्यां भीमो नाटकानां शालामगच्छत्कीचकेन सह अमिलच्च।

10. तयोर्युद्धमासीद्भीमः कीचकस्य देहमनाशयच्च॥

उक्तवान् (m)   said   उक्तवती (f)   said
नाटकः (m)   dancer

CHAPTER NINETEEN

19.1 Epic Civilisation: Stages of Life

The Sanskrit tradition recognises four stages of human life:

Brahmacārin — a student, literally 'walking with the Supreme Being'. The student keeps company with the Supreme Being through study of the scriptures and attending to the teacher.

Gṛhastha — a householder, literally 'staying in a house'. The householder is economically active and fully participates in society, but is advised to be detached in the midst of action.

Vānaprastha — a forest dweller, literally 'set off for the forest'. This means that a a person gives up the household life and is no longer actively participating in economic activity. Time is devoted to spiritual matters.

Saṃnyāsin — a renunciate, literally 'laying down completely'. It is said that this stage can be resorted to at any time. It means giving up all possessions and attachments.

Of these four, the only economically active stage is that of the householder. In this way the other three stages depend on the householder.

19.2 IGCSE Vocabulary 2 — People

ऋषिः (m)	sage
कन्या (f)	daughter
गुरुः (m)	teacher
जनः/जनाः (m)	person / people
जनकः (m)	father
जननी (f)	mother
दुर्जनः (m)	bad person
दूतः (m)	messenger
नरः (m)	man
नारी (f)	lady
नृपः (m)	king
पतिः (m)	husband / lord
पत्नी (f)	wife

EXERCISE 144

Copy in *devanāgarī* each word in the IGCSE vocabulary list (2). Then, against each word, first write it in transliteration and then say what the word means, giving an example of someone in Sanskrit literature who exemplifies it. For example:

ऋषिः   *ṛṣi*   sage   व्यासः

You can also draw a small picture next to each if there is time.

The sage Vyāsa.

19.3 *Ac Sandhi* — the Joining of Vowels

In Sanskrit there are the simple vowels:

अ/आ   इ/ई   उ/ऊ   ऋ/ॠ   (ऌ)

and dipthongs:

ए   ओ   ऐ   औ.

All these vowels and dipthongs are only written in this way at the <u>beginning</u> of words. We never see them in this form in the middle or at the end of a word!

Short अ is invisible in the middle or at the end of a word: it is always sounded after a consonant if there is no halanta. For example:

क = *ka*   क् = *k*

Except for short अ, all other vowels and dipthongs have abbreviated forms in the middle or at the end of a word as follows:

आ	is written	ा	ए	is written	े
इ / ई	are written	ी / ि	ऐ	is written	ै
उ / ऊ	are written	ु / ू	ओ	is written	ो
ऋ / ॠ	are written	ृ / ॄ	औ	is written	ौ

It is very important to remember these abbreviated forms when applying sandhi!

40

RULE 1 OF *AC SANDHI* HAS 4 PARTS:

(a) The first part says:

अ before अ > आ (T)

For example: तत्र आसीत् > तत्रासीत्

(b) The second part says:

ि before इ > ी

For example: नारी इति > नारीति

(c) The third part says:

ु before उ > ू

For example: तु उपरि > तूपरि

(d) The fourth part says:

ृ before ऋ > ॄ

For example: पितृ ऋषिः > पितॄषिः

Note that the vowels being replaced may be short or long.

EXERCISE 145

Write the correct vowel sandhi for each of the following pairs of words in the light of Rule 1 given on the immediately preceding page.

1. अत्र अचलः ....

2. तदा आत्मा ....

3. इति इदानीम् ....

4. साधु उत्तम् ....

5. नारी ईशः ....

6. मातृ ऋषभः ....

7. शिला अश्वः ....

8. साध्वी इच्छति ....

9. तत्र आचार्यः ....

10. विष्णु उपायः ....

RULE 2 OF *AC SANDHI* HAS 2 PARTS:

(a) The first part says:

अ before इ >   े

For example: तत्र इति > तत्रेति

(b) The second part says:

अ before उ > ो

For example: तत्र उत्तमः > तत्रोत्तमः

EXERCISE 146

Write the correct vowel sandhi for each of the following pairs of words in the light of Rule 2 given on the immediately preceding page.

1. अत्र इति ....

2. राम ईशः ....

3. सर्वत्र उद्धरति ....

4. राम उत्तरम् ....

5. अथ इदानीम् ....

6. सीतां उपनिषद् ....

7. यदा इच्छति ....

8. तत्र उपाविशत् ....

Now see if you can take these out of sandhi:

9. तत्रेति ....

10. तत्रोपविश ....

44

RULE 3 OF *AC SANDHI* SAYS:

अ or आ before ऋ > अर्

For example: सीता ऋषिः   >   सीतर्षिः

Note: The long आ always disappears,
leaving a short अर् (अ ॑)

EXERCISE 147

Write the correct vowel sandhi for each of the following pairs of words in the light of Rule 3 given on the immediately preceding page.

1. राम ऋषभः   ....

2. राजा ऋषिः   ....

3. सर्वत्र ऋषयः   ....

4. अरण्य ऋषिः   ....

5. अत्र ऋषभः   ....

6. अभय ऋषिः   ....

7. नर ऋषभः   ....

Now see if you can take these out of sandhi:

8. राक्षसर्षिः   ....

9. दशरथर्षयः   ....

10. एकदर्षभाः   ....

EXERCISE 148

Now write the correct vowel sandhi for each of the following pairs of words in the light of Rules 1, 2 and 3 given on the preceding pages.

1. नाम इति   ....

2. सीता ईशः   ....

3. सर्व उत्तरम्   ....

4. राक्षस उदरम्   ....

5. यदा इदानीम्   ....

6. सीता उत्तिष्ठति   ....

7. अथ इति   ....

8. नर ऋषिः   ....

9. दशरथ ऋषयः   ....

10. एकदा ऋषभः   ....

RULE 4 OF *AC SANDHI* HAS 2 PARTS:

(a) The first part says:

अ / आ before ए or ऐ > ै

For example: अत्र एहि   >   अत्रैहि

तत्र ऐच्छत्   >   तत्रैच्छत्

तदा ऐच्छत्   >   तदैच्छत्

(b) The second part says:

अ / आ before ओ or औ > ौ

For example: अत्र ओषधयः   >   अत्रौषधयः

तत्र औपनिषदा >   तत्रौपनिषदा

तदा ओषधयः   >   तदौषधयः

48

Exercise 149

Write the correct vowel sandhi for each of the following pairs of words in the light of Rule 4 given on the immediately preceding page.

1. अद्य एतत्   ....

2. अचल ओषधयः   ....

3. कदा ऐच्छत्   ....

4. कथा एवम्   ....

5. उवाच औपनिषदः   ....

6. तारका एव   ....

7. अरुण ओषधिम्   ....

8. कन्या एतस्मिन्   ....

Now try to take these out of sandhi:

9. आश्रमौषधयः   ....

10. नैव   ....

Exercise 150

Now write the correct vowel sandhi for each of the following pairs of words in the light of Rules 1, 2, 3 and 4 given on the preceding pages.

1. अधुना एतद्   ....

2. जनक आनन्द   ....

3. भार्या ऐच्छत्   ....

4. इति इदानीम्   ....

5. नासिका उत्तमा   ....

6. न इति   ....

7. सीता ओषधयः   ....

8. इति इच्छति   ....

9. सीता अभवत्   ....

10. अचल ऋषिः   ....

19.4 Vocabulary for Story 19

Note to teacher: Words with an asterisk (*) are part of the IGCSE vocabulary.

NOUNS

*युद्धम्	(n)	battle	*पुत्रः	(m)	son
*कालः	(m)	time	*अन्तः	(m)	end
*लोकः	(m)	world	*रथः	(m)	chariot

ADJECTIVES

*एक॰	one, a certain	*वीर॰	brave
*अन्य॰	another, other	*नष्ट॰	destroyed

INDECLINABLE

*एव	alone

DHĀTUS / VERBS / '-त्वा' ENDINGS

DHĀTUS		VERBS		'-त्वा' ENDINGS	
कृ	in making	*करोति	he makes	कृत्वा	having made
जि	in conquering	*जयति	he conquers	जित्वा	having conquered
प्र + विश्	in entering	*प्रविशति	he enters	प्रविश्य[1]	having entered
वि + आ + पद्	in killing	*व्यापादयति	he kills	व्यापाद्य[1]	having killed

[1] *Notice the -य ending instead of -त्वा.*

19.5 Story 19

ABHIMANYU'S BATTLE PLAN

Droṇa, fighting for the Kauravas, creates a special wheel formation which is lethal. Arjuna, fighting for the Pāṇḍavas, knows how to defeat this formation but is absent. His teenage son, Abhimanyu, volunteers to penetrate the formation. He does so, but no other Pāṇḍavas are able to follow him. After a brave fight, Abhimanyu is killed.

1. कस्मिंश्चिद्युद्धे कौरवो द्रोणश्चक्रव्यूहमकरोत् ।

2. अर्जुन एव चक्रव्यूहं जेष्यतीति पाण्डवा अवदन् ।

3. तस्मिन्नेव काले तु अर्जुनोऽन्यस्मिँल्लोके युद्धमकरोत् ।

4. अर्जुनपुत्रोऽभिमन्युर्नाम उक्तवानहमेव चक्रव्यूहं जेष्यामीति ।

5. अभिमन्युश्चक्रव्यूहं प्राविशत् ।

6. न कश्चनान्यः पाण्डवस्तु चक्रव्यूहं प्राविशत् ।

[continues on page 54]

चक्रव्यूहम्   wheel formation

52

Abhimanyu breaks into the wheel formation.

[continued from page 52]

7. बहुकौरवा अभिमन्युना सह युद्धमकुर्वन् ।

8. वीरोऽभिमन्युर्बहून्कौरवान्व्यापादयत् ।

9. अन्ते तु अभिमन्यो* रथो नष्टः ।

10. स बालकः सर्वैः कौरवैर्हतः ॥

* *Visarga before halanta* र् *is removed (and a preceding* अ, इ *or* उ *is lengthened).*

EXERCISE 151

Having read through the preceding story carefully, do not write out a translation, but answer in English the following questions. Give Sanskrit names in transliteration.

1. On which side was Droṇa fighting? (line 1)

2. What was the name of the battle formation that Droṇa made, and what does does the Sanskrit name of the formation literally mean? (line 1)

3. Translate *'arjuna eva cakravyūhaṃ jeṣyatīti pāṇḍavā avadan'*. (line 2)

4. Who was Abhimanyu, and what did he volunteer to do? (line 4)

5. Translate *'vīro'bhimanyur bahūn kauravān vyāpādayat'*. (line 8)

6. What happened to Abhimanyu's chariot? (line 9)

7. Translate *'sa bālakaḥ sarvaiḥ kauravair hataḥ'*. (line 10)

CHAPTER TWENTY

20.1 Epic Civilisation: Priests and Kings

In Sanskrit literature, the relationship between priests and kings is important. The priests are called *brāhmaṇa* (literally one who knows Brahman, the spirit) and the kings are called *kṣatriya* (those who have worldly power).

It is said that the *kṣatriya* should respect the *brāhmaṇa*, for the *kṣatriya* relies on the *brāhmaṇa* for wisdom. Yet the *brāhmaṇa* should also respect the *kṣatriya*, for the *brāhmaṇa* relies on the *kṣatriya* for protection. In Story 20, Karṇa is a *kṣatriya* who pretends to be a *brāhmaṇa*.

A brāhmaṇa annoints a kṣatriya as king at a coronation ceremony.

We have so far learned the first four rules of ac sandhi.
In this chapter we shall look at the remaining Rules 5 to 7.

RULE 5 OF *AC SANDHI* HAS 3 PARTS:

(**V** = Vowel)

(a) The first part says:

ि or ी before **V** > य् joined to **V**

For example: भवति आस्यम्   > भवत्यास्यम्

(b) The second part says:

ु or ू before **V**   >   व् joined to **V**

For example: साधु इति   >   साध्विति

(c) The third part says:

ृ or ॄ before **V**   >   ्(र्) joined to **V**

For example: पितृ उपविशति   >   पित्रुपविशति

Note that Rule 1 takes precedence over this rule,
so इति इदम् > इतीदम् not इत्यिदम्.

*Also note that the य् व् and र् (्) **must be attached***
to the consonant before it.

EXERCISE 152

Write the correct vowel sandhi for each of the following pairs of words in the light of *ac sandhi* Rule 5 given on the immediately preceding page.

1. अपि अत्र　　　　...

2. साधु आनन्दः　...

3. मधु इच्छति　　...

4. मणि उत्तिष्ठति　...

5. भ्रातृ इति　　　...

6. नदी आत्मा　　...

7. तु इति　　　　...

8. लघु आचार्यः　...

9. अस्ति अथ　　...

10. मातृ औषधयः　...

EXERCISE 153

Write the correct vowel sandhi for each of the following pairs of words in the light of *ac sandhi* Rules 1, 2, 3, 4 and 5:

1. अथ ऋषभः   ....

2. इति आसीत्   ....

3. यदा ऋहि   ....

4. पितृ एतद्   ....

5. तत्र ऐच्छत्   ....

6. भार्या औत्तरा   ....

7. बालिका ओषधयः   ....

8. साधु इति   ....

9. गुरु उपविशति   ....

10. राम आसन्   ....

RULE 6 OF *AC SANDHI* HAS 2 PARTS:

(*The symbol ऽ is called an 'avagraha' and always represents a short अ. It is never sounded.*)

(a) The first part of this Rule says:

े before अ > ेऽ

For example: रामे अथ > रामेऽथ

(b) The second part says:

ो before अ > ोऽ

For example: गुरो अपि > गुरोऽपि

EXERCISE 154

Write the correct vowel sandhi for each of the following pairs of words in the light of *ac sandhi* Rule 6 given on the immediately preceding page.

1. रामे अचरत्   ....

2. वायो अत्र   ....

3. सर्पे अश्वः   ....

4. धात्रे अस्ति   ....

5. शान्तनो अपि   ....

6. वृद्धे अपि   ....

7. शान्तनो अचलः   ....

8. द्रोणे अवगच्छति   ....

9. सीते इदानीम्   ....

10. पशो उत्तिष्ठति   ....

EXERCISE 155

Write the correct vowel sandhi for each of the following pairs of words in the light of *ac sandhi* Rules 5 and 6:

1. बहु आसीत्   ....

2. सुन्दरी अश्वः   ....

3. धातृ आत्मा   ....

4. खगे अथ   ....

5. बहु एव   ....

6. खादति आगच्छति   ....

7. साधु अगच्छत्   ....

8. वने अश्वः   ....

9. मातृ उदरम्   ....

10. दण्डो अपि   ....

RULE 7 OF *AC SANDHI* HAS 4 PARTS:

(**V** = Vowel — except short अ)

(a) The first part says:

े before **V** > अ before **V**

For example: रामे इति > राम इति

(b) The second part says:

ै before **V** > आ before **V**

For example: तस्मै आसीत् > तस्मा आसीत्

(c) The third part says:

ो before **V** > अ before **V**

For example: गुरो उद्यानम् > गुर उद्यानम्

(d) The fourth part says:

ौ before **V** > आव् joined to **V**

For example: गुरौ उद्यानम् > गुरावुद्यानम्

EXERCISE 156

Write the correct vowel sandhi for each of the following pairs of words in the light of *ac sandhi* Rule 7 given on the immediately preceding page.

1. गुरो आस्यम्   ....

2. नद्यै आसीत्   ....

3. हरौ अभवत्   ....

4. रामे इति   ....

5. रामौ एहि   ....

6. हरे उपगच्छति   ....

7. गुरो आनन्दः   ....

8. सीते एवम्   ....

9. नरौ इति   ....

10. तस्मै अस्मिन्   ....

EXERCISE 157

Write the correct vowel sandhi for each of the following pairs of words in the light of *ac sandhi* Rules 6 and 7:

1. बालकौ इति ....

2. रामे आस्यम् ....

3. सीतायै आत्मा ....

4. वने आदयः ....

5. खगौ एकः ....

6. खगे इति ....

7. तारकायै एव ....

8. अग्नये अन्नम् ....

9. मित्रे अगच्छत् ....

10. तस्मै अभवत् ....

EXERCISE 158

Write the correct vowel sandhi for each of the following pairs of words in the light of *ac sandhi* Rules 1 to 7:

1. बहु एव   ....

2. हरौ इदम्   ....

3. सीतायै आत्मा   ....

4. मातृ ऋषिः   ....

5. न एव   ....

6. खादति आगच्छत्   ....

7. रामे अत्र   ....

8. तदा ओषधिः   ....

9. महा ऋषिः   ....

10. नदी इच्छति   ....

20.3 Mixed *Ac Sandhi* Exercises

All the following exercises relate to *ac sandhi* Rules 1 to 7. Some require the application of sandhi, others ask for the *viyoga* forms of words already in sandhi.

EXERCISE 159

Give the *viyoga* forms of the following pairs of words:

1. अत्रैव ....

2. इतीच्छति ....

3. नगर इति ....

4. नगरेऽभवत् ....

5. अथास्ति ....

6. तस्मा इदम् ....

7. सीतोत्तिष्ठ ....

8. महर्षिः ....

9. गुराविति ....

10. बहूत्तमाः ....

EXERCISE 160

Give the *viyoga* forms of the following pairs of words:

1. कठ्युपनिषद्   ....

2. अथोपाविशत्   ....

3. अद्वैतत्   ....

4. साध्वासीत्   ....

5. तदात्मना   ....

6. बालकाविति   ....

7. तदैच्छत्   ....

8. सुन्दर्यभवत्   ....

9. खगैवम्   ....

10. धात्रात्मा   ....

EXERCISE 161

Give the *viyoga* forms of the following pairs of words:

1. सीतैव ....

2. साध्विदम् ....

3. फल इति ....

4. त्वन्नम् ....

5. कुत्रर्षिः ....

6. नदीति ....

7. नरेष्विदम् ....

8. वेति ....

9. अस्त्यचलः ....

10. तदोत्तमः ....

EXERCISE 162

Apply *ac sandhi* to the following and then give the Rule number:

<u>Rule No.</u>

1. अत्र अचलः ....

2. कपि उपनिषद् ....

3. अथ उपाविशत् ....

4. अत्र एतद् ....

5. साधु आत्मा ....

6. तदा आत्मा ....

7. एव ओषधयः ....

8. बालकौ इति ....

9. इति इदानीम् ....

10. तदा ऐच्छन् ....

11. नर ऋषिः ....

12. सुन्दरी अभवत् ....

13. साधु उदरम् ....

14. खगा एवम् ....

15. धातृ अचलः ....

16. एव इति ....

17. तदा ऋषभः ....

18. विष्णु आस्यम् ....

19. नारी ईशः ....

20. रामे अस्ति ....

[continues next page]

Rule No.

21. बहु एव ....

22. यत्र इदम् ....

23. सीतायै आत्मा ....

24. मातृ ऋषिः ....

25. न एव ....

26. खादति आगच्छत् ....

27. गुरो अत्र ....

28. तदा एति ....

29. हरे अचलः ....

30. नदी इच्छति ....

31. महा ऋषिः ....

32. वने उपगच्छति ....

33. गगन आकाशः ....

34. गुरो इति ....

35. क्षुधा उत्तमः ....

36. उवाच एकदा ....

37. धातृ ईशः ....

38. गुरु उत्तरम् ....

39. अहो* इति ....

40. अस्ति इदम् ....

* *Sandhi is not applied to the final vowel of* अहो. *The sandhi is 'held back'. This is an exception to rules 6 (b) and 7 (c).*

EXERCISE 163

Apply *viyoga* to the following *ac sandhi* words, and then give the Rule number:

		Rule No.
1. कन्येति	....	....
2. अत्रर्षिः	....	....
3. जननीति	....	....
4. एकदाश्वः	....	....
5. भार्यैवम्	....	....
6. रात्र्यन्तः	....	....
7. बलिष्ठेति	....	....
8. अथैवम्	....	....
9. गुर्वश्वः	....	....
10. गुरूत्तमः	....	....
11. शालैव	....	....
12. रात्रावासीत्	....	....
13. इतीदम्	....	....
14. त्विति	....	....
15. अथाचिरेण	....	....
16. राजर्षिः	....	....
17. नार्युवाच	....	....
18. तदोत्तिष्ठ	....	....
19. कन्यैकदा	....	....
20. गज उपविश	....	....

20.4 Mixed *Ac* and *Hal Sandhi*

The exercise on the next page relates to *ac* and *hal sandhi* using all rules:

EXERCISE 164

Apply *ac* or *hal sandhi* to the following:

1. भार्या इच्छति ....

2. रामात् अस्ति ....

3. अस्ति इति ....

4. आसन् शालाः ....

5. तत् लभते ....

6. इति आसीत् ....

7. अचले अस्ति ....

8. अखादत् मत्स्यः ....

9. अत्र उवाच ....

10. अनाशयत् हस्तः ....

11. तर्हि इदानीम् ....

12. तत् च ....

13. अपतन् इव ....

14. गुरो अवदत् ....

15. अभवम् कुतः ....

16. तदा ऋषिः ....

17. नृपात् कपिः ....

18. अभवत् भयम् ....

[continues next page]

[continued]

19. आसीत् जनकः ....

20. रामे आसीत् ....

Karṇa forgets a special mantra when most in need of it.

20.5 Vocabulary for Story 20

*Note to teacher: Words with an asterisk (*) are part of the IGCSE vocabulary.*

NOUNS

*शरः (m) arrow   *कर्णः (m) ear

*धर्मः (m) righteousness, justice

ADJECTIVES

*कृत° made / did   *धार्मिक° righteous, just

INDECLINABLES

*सह (+ 3rd) together with   *पुनः[1]   again

*प्रति (+ 3rd) towards   *ततः   after that, therefore, hence

*एव only, indeed, exactly *अपि   also, even

*तु but, now, verily   *पूर्वम् (+ 5th) before

*तस्मात् therefore

DHĀTUS		VERBS		'-त्वा' ENDINGS	
क्षिप्	in throwing	*क्षिपति	he throws	क्षिप्त्वा	having thrown
तुद्	in hitting	*तुदति	he hits	तुत्त्वा	having hit
निर् + गम्	in going out	*निर्गच्छति	he goes out	निर्गम्य[2]	having gone out
स्था	in standing	*तिष्ठति	he stands	स्थित्वा	having stood
श्रु	in hearing	*शृणोति	he hears	श्रुत्वा	having heard

---

[1] पुनः *will appear as* पुनर् *in sandhi before vowels and soft consonants.*

[2] *Notice the* -य *ending instead of* -त्वा.

20.6 Story 20

ARJUNA DEFEATS KARṆA

Karṇa was a *kṣatriya*. When he wanted to be given special training in weapons by Bhārgava, he lied to Bhārgava, maintaining he was a *brāhmaṇa*. Bhārgava hated *kṣatriyas,* and would not have taught Karṇa if he had known the truth. As we heard in Story 14, when Bhārgava discovered the lie he cursed Karṇa. The curse was that the special mantra which Bhārgava had taught Karṇa would be forgotten when Karṇa most needed it. In the story in this chapter, when Karṇa meets Arjuna in battle, at the crucial moment Karṇa cannot remember the mantra which could have defeated Arjuna.

1. अर्जुनः कर्णेन सह युद्धमकरोत्।

2. कर्णोऽर्जुनस्य <u>शिरः</u> प्रति शरमक्षिपत्।

3. तस्मिन्नेव काले तु कृष्णस्य माययार्जुनस्य रथः पङ्के <u>निमग्नः</u>।

4. तस्मात्कर्णस्य शरोऽर्जुनस्य <u>शिरो</u> नातुदत्।

5. रथस्तु तस्मात्पङ्कात्पुनर्निरगच्छत्।

[story continues on page 78]

शिरस् (n)	head	निमग्न° (mfn)	sunk
पङ्कः (m)	mud		

76

Arjuna kills Karṇa.

[story continued from page 76]

6. ततः कर्णस्य रथोऽपि पङ्के निमग्नः।

7. रथस्य चक्रं पङ्केऽतिष्ठत्।

8. कर्णो रथादवरुह्यार्जुनमवदच्छरं न क्षिपेति।

9. अर्जुनेन युद्धस्य धर्मो ज्ञातः।

10. ततः स न किंचिदकरोत्।

11. कृष्णोऽर्जुनमवदत्पूर्वं धर्मः कर्णेन न कदापि कृतः।

12. धर्मो धार्मिकमेव नरं रक्षतीति।

13. तच्छ्रुत्वार्जुनः कर्णं व्यापादयत्॥

चक्रम् (n)	wheel	न किंचित्	nothing
अवरोहति	climbs down	न कदापि	never
ज्ञात° (mfn)	known		

CHAPTER TWENTY-ONE

21.1 Epic Civilisation: Merit and Demerit

The Sanskrit tradition speaks of the merit and demerit accumulated through action. By performing good, lawful actions one accumulates पुण्य (merit). By performing evil, unlawful actions one accumulates पाप (demerit). Those who accumulate पुण्य go to heaven, and those who accumulate पाप go to hell. In the story in this chapter, Duryodhana points out that Bhīma performs an unlawful action when he strikes him (Duryodhana) on the thighs, which was against the laws of battle. Duryodhana therefore says that only he will go to heaven, not Bhīma.

Bhīma strikes Duryodhana's thighs.

21.2 IGCSE Vocabulary 3 (More People)

पितृ (m)	father
पुत्रः (m)	son
पुरुषः (m)	person
बालकः (m)	boy
भर्तृ (m)	husband
भार्या (f)	wife
भृत्यः (m)	servant
भ्रातृ (m)	brother
मनुष्यः (m)	man
मातृ (f)	mother
मित्रम् (n)	friend
मुनिः (m)	sage

EXERCISE 165

Below are some 'Who am I?' puzzles. The solutions are the words given in the vocabulary on the preceding page. Give the answers in *devanāgarī*.

1. *Clues:* I can be either male or female.
   I will stand by you in good and bad times.
   I see you at school.
   Who am I? ....

2. *Clues:* I am the earth.
   I measure out all things.
   I am the person who gave birth to you.
   Who am I? ....

3. *Clues:* I am wise.
   I can offer you good advice.
   I meditate.
   Who am I? ....

4. *Clues:* I can be older or younger.
   I can also be the same age.
   I have the same mother as you.
   Who am I? ....

5. *Clues:* I am young.
   I am male.
   I am full of potential.
   Who am I? ....

6. *Clues:* I am Spirit.
   I am being.
   I am sometimes a human being.
   Who am I? ....

21.3 Separating Words in Writing

Words in *sandhi* join at the top line — except when:

1. There is a vowel at the end of the first word and a consonant at the beginning of the second word.

>   Example: इति रामः

2. There is an *anusvāra* at the end of the first word.

>   Example: रामं तत्

3. *Visarga* has not been lost through sandhi, i.e. before क्, ख्, प्, फ्, श्, ष्, स्

>   Example: रामः पतति

4. There is a gap created by *sandhi*.

>   Examples: रामाः आसन्   >   रामा आसन्
>   रामे इति   >   राम इति

5. In *sandhi,* no *halanta* signs are allowed except at the very end of a sentence. Consonants join together whether there is a *sandhi* change or not.

>   Example: रामात् सन्ति   >   रामात्सन्ति

82

EXERCISE 166

Join the following, applying the correct sandhi, if necessary:

1. सीतां मम   > ....

2. सीताम् इति   > ....

3. रथान् चरति   > ....

4. ऋषिः मया   > ....

5. रामान् पतित्वा > ....

6. रामात् सन्ति   > ....

7. शालाः शशकः   > ....

8. रामे अस्ति   > ....

9. मित्रे ऋषिः   > ....

10. कन्याः नाशयति > ....

21.4 Summaries of the Three Types of Sandhi

(a) Visarga Sandhi

End of First Word	Beginning of Second Word (Hard Letters)	Final Form	Examples
Any final *visarga* (no matter what precedes)	(a) क् ख् प् फ् श् ष् स्	remains the same *(visarga)*	रामः खादति > रामः खादति
	(b) त्	स्	रामः तत् > रामस्तत्
	(c) च् or छ्	श्	रामः च > रामश्च

End of First Word	Beginning of Second Word (Soft Letters)	Final Form	Examples
अः	(a) अ	ओऽ	रामः अत्र > रामोऽत्र
	(b) any vowel except अ	अ	रामः एव > राम एव
	(c) any soft letter except अ	ओ	रामः मम > रामो मम
आः	any soft consonant	आ	रामाः हि > रामा हि
any final *visarga* (except for those preceded by अः and आः)	any vowel or soft consonant	र्	ऋषिः एव > ऋषिरेव गुरुः माम् > गुरुर्माम्
The words सः (he, that) and एषः (this) before any consonant lose their *visarga*.			

84

(b) Consonant Sandhi

End of First Word	Beginning of Second Word	Final Form	Examples
त्	(a) क् ख् त् प् फ् स्	त्	तत् कर्म > तत्कर्म तत् तत् > तत्तत्
	(b) any vowel or soft consonant *[except for (c) to (h) immediately below]*	द्	तत् अयम् > तदयम् तत् एव > तदेव तत् यदा > तद्यदा तत् वा > तद्वा तत् रामः > तद्रामः तत् धर्मः > तद्धर्मः तत् भव > तद्भव तत् गजः > तद्गजः
	(c) च्	च्	तत् च > तच्च
	(d) ज्	ज्	तत् जलम् > तज्जलम्
	(e) न् म्	न्	तत् नाम > तन्नाम तत् मम > तन्मम
	(f) ल्	ल्	तत् लोकः > तल्लोकः
	(g) श्	both replaced by च्छ्	तत् श्रुत्वा > तच्छुत्वा
	(h) ह्	both replaced by द्ध्	तत् हस्तः > तद्धस्तः
न्	(a) च्	both replaced by ँश्च्	तान् च > तांश्च
	(b) त्	both replaced by ँस्त्	तान् तदा > तांस्तदा
	(c) ज् श्	ञ्	तान् जलम् > ताञ्जलम्
	(d) ल्	ँल्ँ	तान् लीला > ताल्ँलीला
इन्/अन्	(e) any vowel	इन्न्/अन्न्	अभवन् उत्तमाः > अभवन्नुत्तमाः
म्	any consonant	*anusvāra*	राममम् खगः > रामं खगः

(c) Vowel Sandhi

End of First Word	Beginning of Second Word	Final Form	Examples
अ आ इ ई उ ऊ ऋ ॠ	अ आ इ ई उ ऊ ऋ ॠ	both are replaced by आ both are replaced by ई both are replaced by ऊ both are replaced by ॠ	अत्र अस्ति > अत्रास्ति गच्छति इति > गच्छतीति तु उत्तमः > तूत्तमः पितृ ऋषिः > पितॄषिः
अ आ	इ ई	both are replaced by ए	अथ इदम् > अथेदम् तदा इति > तदेति
	उ ऊ	both are replaced by ओ	अथ उपरि > अथोपरि यदा उत्तिष्ठ > यदोत्तिष्ठ
	ऋ ॠ	both are replaced by अर्	अत्र ऋषिः > अत्रर्षिः यदा ऋषभः > यदर्षभः
	ए ऐ	both are replaced by ऐ	अत्र एव > अत्रैव अथ ऐच्छत् > अथैच्छत्
	ओ औ	both are replaced by औ	अत्र ओदनम् > अत्रौदनम् यदा औचित्यम् > यदौचित्यम्
इ ई	a vowel (not इ, ई)	य्	इति एव > इत्येव
उ ऊ	a vowel (not उ, ऊ)	व्	तु अपि > त्वपि
ऋ ॠ	a vowel (not ऋ, ॠ)	र्	पितृ उक्तः > पित्रुक्तः
ए	अ	both are replaced by एऽ	रामे अपि > रामेऽपि
	a vowel other than अ	अ	रामे उक्तः > राम उक्तः
ओ	अ	both are replaced by ओऽ	
	a vowel other than अ	अ	गुरो इति > गुर इति
ऐ	a vowel	आ	तस्मै एव > तस्मा एव
औ	a vowel	आव्	सेवकौ उभौ > सेवकावुभौ

86

EXERCISE 167

Apply sandhi to the following two stories (A) and (B) taken from the beginning of the Mahābhārata course:

(A)

1. आसीत् नृपः शान्तनुः नाम।

2. सः अतीव साधुः नृपः सुखेन अजीवत्।

3. तस्य तु एकः दोषः।

4. तस्य दोषः कामः।

5. एकदा शान्तनुः नद्याः समीपे अचरत्।

6. सः नार्या सह अमिलत्।

7. सा नारी देवी गङ्गा नाम।

8. सा अतीव सुन्दरी नारी।

9. मम भार्या भव दयया इति शान्तनुः अवदत्।

10. गङ्गा अवदत् अहम् तव भार्या भविष्यामि।

11. किम् करोषि इति न कदापि माम् पृच्छ।

12. यदि तत् पृच्छसि तर्हि त्वाम् त्यजामि इति॥

Gaṅgā leaves Śāntanu.

(B)

1. शान्तनुः गङ्गाम् पर्यणयत्।

2. अचिरेण गङ्गायाः पुत्रः आसीत्।

3. सा तु पुत्रम् नद्याम् अक्षिपत्।

4. शान्तनुः तत् अपश्यत्।

5. एवम् गङ्गा सप्त पुत्रान् नद्याम् अक्षिपत्।

6. ते सर्वे मृताः अभवन्।

7. अचिरेण गङ्गायाः अष्टमः पुत्रः आसीत्।

8. सा पुत्रम् नदीम् अनयत्।

9. शान्तनुः तु किम् करोषि इति अपृच्छत्।

10. गङ्गा अवदत् इदानीम् त्वाम् त्यजामि।

11. तव अष्टमः पुत्रः मया सह आगमिष्यति इति॥

EXERCISE 168

Translate these two stories (A) and (B), which you have translated earlier in the Mahābhārata course. They are in sandhi.

(A)

1. शान्तनोरष्टमः पुत्रो भीष्मो नाम ।

2. एकदा भीष्मः शान्तनुमागच्छत् ।

3. त्वमेव नृपो भविष्यसीति शान्तनुर्भीष्মमवदत् ।

4. एकदा तु शान्तनुर्नद्यास्तीरेऽचरत् ।

5. वायौ सुगन्थ आसीत् ।

6. स सुगन्थः सुन्दर्याः कन्याया आगच्छत् ।

7. यत्र यत्र सा नार्यगच्छत्तत्र तत्र सुगन्थ आसीत् ।

8. कन्यां दृष्ट्वा का त्वमिति शान्तनुरपृच्छत् ।

9. कन्यावददहं सत्यवती नाम ।

10. मम जनको धीवराणां नृपोऽस्तीति ॥

(B)

1. धीवराणां नृपं गत्वा शान्तनुः पृच्छति स्म।

2. तव कन्यां विवाह इच्छामीति।

3. धीवराणां नृपः प्रतिवदति स्म यदि सत्यवती तव भार्या भविष्यति तर्हि तस्याः पुत्रो नृपो भविष्यतीति।

4. शान्तनू राजगृहं दुःखेन पुनरगच्छत्।

5. भीष्मः सर्वं श्रुत्वा धीवराणां नृपं गत्वा तं वदति स्म।

6. पुरा शान्तनुर्मामवदद्धे भीष्म त्वं नृपो भविष्यसीति।

7. इदानीं तु सत्यवत्याः पुत्रो नृपो भविष्यति।

8. अहं नृपो न भविष्यामीति मम व्रतम्।

9. शान्तनुः सत्यवतीं परिणयति स्म॥

21.5 Vocabulary for Story 21

Note to teacher: Words with an asterisk (*) are part of the IGCSE vocabulary.

NOUNS

*मातृ	(f)	mother	*धर्मः	(m)	righteousness
*भूमिः	(f)	earth, ground	*स्वर्गः	(m)	heaven

ADJECTIVES

*लभ्य°	(mfn)	found
*हत°	(mfn)	killed
*कृत°	(mfn)	made, did

PRONOUN

*अहम्	I

INDECLINABLES

*यदा ... तदा	when ... then	*अचिरेण		soon
*तु	but, now, verily	*सह	(+ 3rd)	together with
*तस्मात्	therefore	*एव		only, indeed, exactly
*अन्ते	in the end	*एवम्		thus, in such a manner

VERBS

*रक्षति	he protects, saves
*युद्धम् + करोति	he does battle
*प्रविशति	he enters
*तुदति	he hits
*पतति	he falls

'-त्वा' ENDINGS

रक्षित्वा	having protected
युद्धम् + कृत्वा	having done battle
प्रविश्य[1]	having entered
तुत्त्वा	having hit
पतित्वा	having fallen

[1] *Notice the* -य *ending instead of* -त्वा.

21.6 Story 21

DURYODHANA IS SLAIN

Duryodhana's mother, Gāndhārī, had asked Duryodhana to come naked to her. Duryodhana, however, wore a cloth around his thighs. When Gāndhārī removed her blindfold, her eyesight gave special protection to all parts of his body that she could see. Hence, when Duryodhana later met Bhīma in battle, Bhīma was able to defeat Duryodhana by crushing his thighs with a mace.

1. दुर्योधनस्य माता गान्धारी नाम दुर्योधनमुक्तवती नग्नो मामागच्छेति।

2. यदा तु दुर्योधनो गान्धारीमागच्छत्तदोरू* आवृतौ।

3. तस्माद्दुर्योधनस्योरू न रक्षितौ।

4. युद्धस्यान्ते दुर्योधनः कं चिज्जलाशयं प्राविशत्।

5. स तु पाण्डवैरचिरेण लभ्यः।

[continues on page 95]

नग्न°	naked	आवृत°	covered
माम्	to me	जलाशयः (m)	lake
ऊरु (m)	thigh		

* An *ī*, *ū* or *e* when it is a dual ending is held back from *sandhi*.

Bhīma is accused of unlawfully killing Duryodhana.

[continued from page 93]

6. दुर्योधनो भीमेन सह युद्धं कृतवान् ।

7. भीमो दुर्योधनस्योरू <u>गदयातुदत्</u> ।

8. दुर्योधनो भूमावपतद्भीममवदच्च <u>त्वयाधर्मः</u> कृतः ।

9. अहमेव स्वर्गं गमिष्यामीति ।

10. एवं दुर्योधनो भीमेन हतः ॥

गदा (f)	mace, club	अधर्मः (m)	unlawful act
त्वया	by you		

CHAPTER TWENTY-TWO

22.1 Epic Civilisation: Virtues

Virtues are often spoken of and vividly illustrated in the Sanskrit epics. Kṛṣṇa clearly exemplifies these virtues, particularly अक्रोधः, absence of anger. Despite the terrible atrocities in the battles of the Mahābhārata, Kṛṣṇa remains free from anger — even when he is cursed. This enables him to act very effectively to protect the good. In the story in this chapter, for example, he protects Arjuna's unborn grandson. Here are some others of the virtues spoken of:

अहिंसा	harmlessness of thought, speech and action;	दमः	control of mind, senses, speech and body;
सत्यम्	unfailingly truthful speech;	स्वाध्यायः	regular study and recitation of the Scriptures;
अस्तेयम्	abstention from theft;		
शौचम्	cleanliness;	शान्तिः	peace, stillness and contentment;
इन्द्रिय-निग्रहः	control of the senses;		
अभयम्	fearlessness;	दया	compassion for all.
दानम्	generosity;		

Droṇa's son unleashes a missile at Arjuna's grandson in the womb.

22.2 Samāsa

The word 'samāsa' means 'compound'. Compounds are very common in English and some other languages. Here are some examples of English compounds.

postcard

briefcase   downstairs

PICKPOCKET

LIPSTICK   blackbird

skyblue

sweetheart   WINDSHIELD

cupboard

upstairs   toothpaste

wisecrack

EXERCISE 169

In your exercise book, write down ten more English compounds.

22.3 Four Types of समास

There are four main types of compound. These are:

        (1) **tatpuruṣa**

        (2) **bahuvrīhi**

        (3) **dvandva**

        (4) **avyayībhāva**

तत्पुरुष	(tatpuruṣa)	—	NOUN + NOUN NOUN + PPP ADJECTIVE + NOUN
बहुव्रीहि	(bahuvrīhi)	—	any *samāsa* which ends in a noun and is used as an adjective
द्वन्द्व	(dvandva)	—	A LIST
अव्ययीभाव	(avyayībhāva)	—	PREFIX + NOUN ADVERB + NOUN

EXERCISE 170

In your exercise book, write out the table above.

Examples of the four main types

तत्पुरुष	(tatpuruṣa)	— वनखगः	a bird **in** the forest
		नगरगतꞏ	gone **to** town
		दीर्घनासिका	a long nose
बहुव्रीहि	(bahuvrīhi)	— दीर्घनासिकः	(he who has) a long nose
द्वन्द्व	(dvandva)	— नरनारिदेवाः	men, women and gods
अव्ययीभाव	(avyayībhāva)	— यथाकालम्	according to time
		प्रतिहरि	towards the Lord

Exercise 171

In your exercise book, say what type of compound each of the following is.
For example: प्रतिहरि 'towards the Lord' — अव्ययीभाव (avyayībhāva).

1. यथाकालम्   'according to time'

2. यथाकामम्   'according to desire'

3. नरनारिदेवाः   'men, women and gods'

4. सिंहगजमृगाः   'lions, elephants and deer'

5. वनखगः   'a bird in the forest'

6. दीर्घनासिकः   '(he who has) a long nose'

7. देवानन्दः   'the bliss of the gods'

8. दीर्घग्रीवा   '(she who has) a long neck'

9. नगरगत॰   'gone to town'

10. गुरुदृष्ट॰   'seen by the teacher'

22.4 Tatpuruṣa

Perhaps the most common compound is *tatpuruṣa*.

There are five main types of

तत्पुरुष

(1) STANDARD

(translate backwards using to, by, for, from, of or in between the two words)

noun + noun

e.g. वनखगः   'forest-bird (bird **in** the forest)'

noun + ppp

e.g. नगरगत॰   'town-gone (gone **to** the town)'

(2) KARMADHĀRAYA

adjective + noun

e.g. दीर्घनासिका   'long-nose (a nose **which is** long)'

(3) UPAMĀNA

noun + adjective   *(a comparison)*

e.g. गगननील॰   'sky-blue (blue **like** the sky)'

(4) NAÑ

अ / अन् + noun or adjective

e.g. अधर्मः   'injustice'

(5) DVIGU

number + noun

e.g. त्रिलोकम्   'the three worlds'

(At present we shall only consider a neuter singular dvigu, showing a grouping.)

EXERCISE 172

In your exercise book, write out in Sanskrit and English the four main types of *tatpuruṣa* compounds, along with their characteristics and examples.

EXERCISE 173

Here are some *tatpuruṣa* compounds in Sanskrit and English. In your exercise book, copy each compound, draw a vertical dotted line to separate the elements of the compound, and say what type each is. For example:

वन⋮खगः 'forest bird' (standard *tatpuruṣa*).

1. नदीतीरम्　'bank of a river'

2. नीलखगः　'blue bird'

3. त्रिकालम्　'the three times'

4. गगननील॰　'blue like the sky'

5. अज्ञानम्　'ignorance'

6. अचलवनम्　'forest on the mountain'

7. त्रिलोकम्　'the three worlds'

8. ज्येष्ठकन्या　'the eldest daughter'

9. अमृत॰　'not dead, immortal'

10. मित्रप्रिय॰　'dear like a friend'

22.5 Bahuvrīhi

The next most common compound is the *bahuvrīhi*.

बहुव्रीहि

THIS IS <u>ANY SAMĀSA</u> USED AS AN <u>ADJECTIVE</u>

as in the phrase

नरः   सुन्दर-कन्यः
'A man   (with) a beautiful daughter'

Notice here how the feminine word कन्या has taken on a masculine ending (ः) because the compound is describing a masculine word. This proves that the compound is a *bahuvrīhi* and not a *tatpuruṣa*. *Bahuvrīhi* compounds normally end in a noun.

Exercise 174

In your exercise book, translate the following phrases which include *bahuvrīhi* compounds:

1. दीर्घकर्णः कुक्कुरः

2. दीर्घग्रीवा नारी

3. महाकर्णः गजः

4. सुन्दररूपा*

5. प्रबलबाहुः बालकः

6. दीर्घकर्णः*

7. दीर्घग्रीवा*

8. महाकर्णः*

9. सुन्दररूपः*

10. प्रबलबाहुः*

---

*Note: Sometimes a *bahuvrīhi* stands on its own — for example:

जितकामः 'a man who has conquered desire'
जितकामा 'a woman who has conquered desire'

22.6 Dvandva

Less common is the *dvandva* compound.

द्वन्द्व

*This compound takes a **dual ending** if there are
two items listed,*

<u>as in</u>

रात्रि-दिने   'night (and) day'

*or takes a **plural ending** if there are three or more items listed,*

<u>as in</u>

कन्या-पुत्र-जनक-मातरः
'daughters-sons-fathers (and) mothers'

EXERCISE 175

In your exercise book, translate the following *dvandva* compounds:

1. नरनारिदेवाः

2. चन्द्रसूर्यौ

3. पुत्रकन्याः

4. सिंहमूषिकखगाः

5. सुखदुःखे

22.7 Avyayībhāva

Perhaps the most infrequently used compound is the *avyayībhāva*.

अव्ययीभाव

These compounds are always made neuter. The two types are:

PREFIX + NOUN

as in स-स्मितम् 'with a smile'
or प्रति-रात्रि 'each night'

and

ADVERB + NOUN

as in यथा-गुरु 'according to the teacher'

EXERCISE 176

In your exercise book, translate the following *avyayībhāva* compounds:

1. यथाकामम्

2. यावज्जीवम्

3. प्रतिदिनम्

4. उपाग्नि

5. सकोपम्

22.8 Vocabulary for Story 22

NOUNS

पुत्रः	(m)	son	ऋषिः (m)	sage
दुःखम्	(n)	sorrow	शरः (m)	arrow

ADJECTIVES

दृष्ट°	seen		हत°	killed
रक्षित°	protected		मृत°	dead
नष्ट°	ruined, destroyed			

INDECLINABLES

तस्मात्	therefore		एवम्	thus
-अर्थम्	*(at end of compound)* for the sake of		पुनर्	again
प्रति	towards (+ 2nd)			

DHĀTUS

वि + आ + पद्	in killing
अनु + धाव्	in running after
क्षिप्	in throwing, shooting
जि	in conquering
दा	in giving
वद्	in speaking
चिन्त्	in thinking

VERBS

व्यापादयति	he kills
अनुधावति	he runs after
क्षिपति	he shoots
जयति	he conquers
ददाति	he gives
वदति	he speaks
चिन्तयति	he thinks

'-त्वा' ENDINGS

व्यापाद्य[1]	having killed
अनुधाव्य[1]	having run after
क्षिप्त्वा	having shot
जित्वा	having conquered
दत्त्वा	having given
उदित्वा	having spoken
चिन्तयित्वा	having thought

[1] *Notice the* -य *ending instead of* -त्वा.

22.9   Story 22

DROṆA'S SON TRIES TO DESTROY THE CHILD IN UTTARĀ'S WOMB

Droṇa's son kills Draupadī's children. The Pāṇḍavas pursue him. Droṇa's son releases a missile aimed at the child in Uttarā's womb, who is Arjuna's unborn grandson. Kṛṣṇa counteracts the force of the missile. The Pāṇḍavas kill Droṇa's son, and remove a jewel from his forehead, which is given to Draupadī.

1. द्रोणपुत्रो द्रौपदीपुत्रान्व्यापादयत् ।

2. तस्मात्पाण्डवानां दुःखमासीत् ।

3. ते द्रोणपुत्रमन्वधावन् ।

4. स तु ऋषिं व्यासं रक्षार्थमगच्छच्छरमुत्तरागर्भं

   प्रत्यक्षिपच्च ।

5. उत्तरागर्भेऽर्जुनप्रपुत्र आसीत् ।

[continues on page 110]

रक्षार्थम्	for protection	प्रति (+ 2nd case ending)	towards
गर्भः (m)	womb	प्रपुत्रः (m)	grandson

Kṛṣṇa counteracts the force of the missile directed at Uttarā.

[continued from page 108]

6. कृष्णेन तु शरः दृष्टः उत्तरा रक्षिता च।

7. एवमर्जुनप्रपुत्रो न हतः।

8. पाण्डवा द्रोणपुत्रमजयन्।

9. तस्य ललाटे मणिरासीत्।

10. द्रोणपुत्रो भीमाय मणिमददात्।

11. भीमो मणिं द्रौपद्यै दत्त्वा द्रोणपुत्रो मृत इति तामवदत्।

12. द्रौपद्या दुःखं तु न नष्टम्।

13. मम पुत्रा हता इति सा पुनः पुनरचिन्तयत्।

14. तया मणिर्युधिष्ठिराय दत्तः॥

ललाटः (m)	forehead	दत्त्वा	having given
मणिः (m)	jewel	नष्ट° (mfn)	destroyed

110

22.10 Sanskrit Crossword Puzzle

Name in transliteration the different types of *samāsa*. Make sure you spell them correctly.

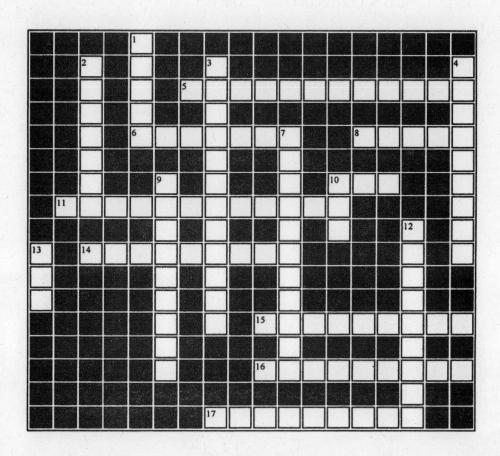

Across	Down
5. black-board (12)	1. the nine planets (5)
6. ink-black (7)	2. gods, men, demons and beasts (7)
8. the three worlds (5)	3. *sādhu-nara* (12)
10. un-righteous (3)	4. she (who is) a tomboy (9)
11. wise-sage (12)	7. *prati-agni* (12)
14. men (who have) intelligent-minds (9)	9. he (who has) blue eyes (9)
15. *nagara-gata* (9)	10. *a-sadhu* ['not good'] (3)
16. the king's-daughter (9)	12. man-seen (9)
17. tiger-eaten (9)	13. un-happy (3)

CHAPTER TWENTY-THREE

23.1 Epic Civilisation: Māyā, the Play of Illusion

The Sanskrit scriptures often describe this world as being māyā — 'illusion'. It is said that we are engaged in a great play, and have all been allotted parts as in a drama. Kṛṣṇa, in the story of the Mahābhārata, is keenly aware of acting out a part within the māyā. Hence, when he is fatally shot by a hunter, he accepts this turn of events in the drama with contentment, knowing that his death was due.

A hunter shoots Kṛṣṇa.

23.2 IGCSE Vocabulary 4 (Even More People)

राक्षसः (m)	demon
राक्षसी (f)	demoness
राजन् (m)	king
राजपुत्रः (m)	prince
राज्ञी (f)	queen
वीरः (m)	hero
शत्रुः (m)	enemy
शिष्यः (m)	pupil
सेवकः (m)	servant
सोदरः (m)	brother
सैनिकः (m)	soldier
स्वसृ (f)	sister
स्वामिन् (m)	master

23.3 The Formation of Compounds

> There are two points to remember
> when forming compounds:
>
> **(1) Only the <u>final</u> word has an ending.**
>
> **(2) All other words are in stem form.**
>
> *For example:* रामसीते 'Rāma and Sītā'

EXERCISE 177

For each of the following Sanskrit compounds, write in your exercise book the stem form of the <u>first</u> member of the compound:

1. कपिमुखम् — the face of a monkey

2. अल्पनासिका — small nose

3. रामसीते — Rāma and Sītā

4. कृष्णखगः — blackbird

5. गगननीलम् — sky blue

6. सप्तसमुद्रम् — the seven oceans

7. गृहद्वारम् — door of the house

8. मृतखगः — a dead bird

9. नरनारीदेवराक्षसाः — men, women, gods and demons

10. प्रतिनगरम् — towards the town

114

23.4 How to Analyse a Compound

How do we analyse a compound with three or more words? Here is an example:

नृपकन्याखादितफलानि

नृप	कन्या	खादित	फलानि
king	daughter	eaten	fruits

(1) Look at the last word फलानि 'fruits' and consider the relationship it forms with the preceding word खादित 'eaten'. Together they mean **'fruits eaten'**.

(2) Next, we find the relationship between this pair of words and the preceding word कन्या 'daughter'. Together they mean **'fruits eaten (by) the daughter'**.

(3) We then take this final group of three words and relate it to the preceding word नृप 'king'. So the whole compound is now seen to mean:

'fruits eaten (by) the daughter (of) the king'

Here is a diagram to illustrate this:

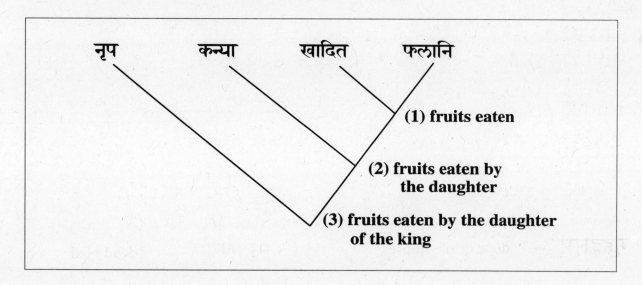

23.5 समास Exercises

EXERCISE 178

(A) Write in, below, the names of the four main types of *samāsa* in *devanāgarī* and in transliteration, making sure that the transliteration is correct.

Transliteration	*Devanāgarī*
1. T	....
2. B	....
3. D	....
4. A	....

(B) Now give the **four main categories of *tatpuruṣa*** compounds in *devanāgarī* and in transliteration, again making sure the transliteration is correct.

Transliteration	*Devanāgarī*
1. Standard T	Standard त...................
2. K	....
3. U	....
4. N	....

116

EXERCISE 179

Write below the meaning and type of each of these compounds:

SAMĀSA	MEANING	TYPE
1. (a) दग्ध-वृक्षः	....	....
(b) अग्नि-दग्ध-वृक्षः	....	
(c) महा-अग्नि-दग्ध-वृक्षः	....	
2. (a) गृह-भूमिः	....	....
(b) राज-गृह-भूमिः	....	
3. (a) पूर्ण-नेत्रम्	....	....
(b) जल-पूर्ण-नेत्रम्	....	
4. (a) जित-भयः	....	....
(b) अ-जित-भयः	....	
5. (a) वचन-आनन्दः	....	....
(b) राम-वचन-आनन्दः	....	
6. (a) संतुष्ट-गजः	....	....
(b) जल-संतुष्ट-गजः	....	
7. (a) तुदित-सर्पः	....	....
(b) ग्राम-नर-तुदित-सर्पः	....	

EXERCISE 180

Draw in a short vertical dotted line to separate the words in each of these *tatpuruṣa* compounds. Then write in the meaning and type of each. The first one is done for you as an example.

SAMĀSA	MEANING	TYPE
1. ऋषि॒ज्ञानम्	'knowledge of the sages'[1]	standard *tatpuruṣa*
2. सप्तसमुद्रम्		
3. सिंहहतः		
4. वृक्षस्थः		
5. महामुनिः		
6. भूमिपतितः		
7. अधार्मिकः		
8. धनागताः		
9. त्रिकालम्		
10. राक्षसकृतम्		
11. सर्पभयम्		
12. वृक्षपर्णम्		

[1] The non-final element in any compound can be singular, dual or plural.

118

EXERCISE 181

In your exercise book, for each of the following sentences name the *bahuvrīhi* compounds and then translate the sentence.

1. गजम् श्रुत्वा वनगताः जनाः दीर्घकर्णः अत्र इति अवदन् ।

2. जितभयाः सैनिकाः नगरम् आगच्छन् ।

3. राक्षसम् दृष्ट्वा लक्ष्मणः महोदरः तत्र अस्ति इति अक्रोशत् ।

4. मुनिः अवदत् अहम् त्यक्तगृहः इति ।

5. हतजनका नारी भूमिम् अपतत् ॥

EXERCISE 182

In your exercise book, translate each of the compounds in the oval and name the type.
For example: जलशुद्धम् 'pure like water' (*upamāna*).

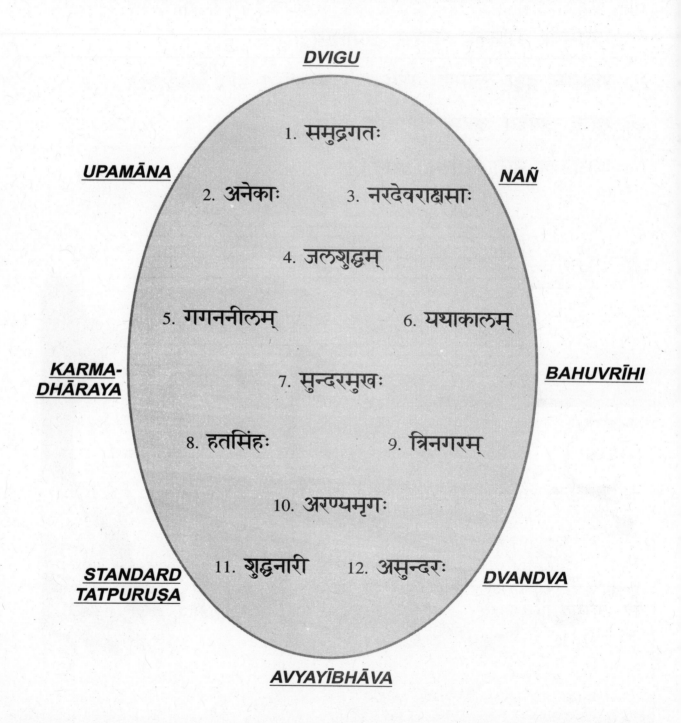

DVIGU

UPAMĀNA

NAÑ

KARMA-
DHĀRAYA

BAHUVRĪHI

STANDARD
TATPURUṢA

DVANDVA

AVYAYĪBHĀVA

1. समुद्रगतः

2. अनेकाः 3. नरदेवराक्षसाः

4. जलशुद्धम्

5. गगननीलम् 6. यथाकालम्

7. सुन्दरमुखः

8. हतसिंहः 9. त्रिनगरम्

10. अरण्यमृगः

11. शुद्धनारी 12. असुन्दरः

23.6 Vocabulary for Story 23

NOUNS

वृक्षः	(m)	tree
पादः	(m)	foot
मृगः	(m)	deer
शरः	(m)	arrow

स्वर्गः	(m)	heaven
धर्मः	(m)	righteousness
ज्ञानम्	(n)	knowledge

ADJECTIVES

दृष्ट°	seen
संतुष्ट°	contented

PRONOUN

एकः	(m)	one, a certain

INDECLINABLES

अधः	beneath
दूरे	far away
शीघ्रम्	quickly
दुःखेन	unhappily

तु	but
तत्र	there
इदानीम्	now

DHĀTU

उप+विश्	in sitting down
चिन्त्	in thinking
अस्	in existing
क्षिप्	in throwing
क्रुश्	in crying out
वि+आ+पद्	in killing
आ+गम्	in coming

VERB

उपविशति	he sits down
चिन्तयति	he thinks
अस्ति	he is, exists
क्षिपति	he throws
क्रोशति	he cries out
व्यापादयति	he kills
आगच्छति	he comes

'-त्वा' ENDING

उपविश्य[1]	having sat down
चिन्तयित्वा	having thought
—	
क्षिप्त्वा	having thrown
क्रुष्ट्वा	having cried out
व्यापाद्य[1]	having killed
आगम्य[1]	having come

[1] *Notice the* -य *ending instead of* -त्वा.

Story 23

> ## KṚṢṆA IS SHOT BY A HUNTER
>
> When Kṛṣṇa lies down, his feet are mistaken by a hunter for the ears of a forest animal. The hunter shoots his arrow, which enters Kṛṣṇa's body. The hunter is horrified on discovering what has happened, but Kṛṣṇa tells him not to fear and assures the hunter that he will go to heaven for the deed, which fulfilled destiny. Kṛṣṇa tells his charioteer that he will now depart from the body and gives him some final advice.

1. कृष्णोऽधोवृक्षमुपाविशत् ।

2. एको व्याधः कृष्णसमीपेऽचरत् ।

3. तेन व्याधेन कृष्णपादावेव दूरे दृष्टौ ।

4. व्याधोऽचिन्तयन्मृगो वृक्षस्याधोऽस्तीति ।

5. व्याधः शरं शीघ्रमक्षिपत् ।

[continues on p.124]

अधः (+ 6th case)	beneath	पादः (m)	foot
व्याधः (m)	hunter		

Kṛṣṇa departs from the body with contentment.

[continued from p. 122]

6. व्याधशरः कृष्णं प्राविशत्।

7. कृष्णमागम्य व्याधो दुःखेनाक्रोशद्धे कृष्ण मां व्यापादयेति।

8. कृष्णस्त्ववदद्धे व्याध अभीतो भव।

9. त्वं स्वर्गं गमिष्यसीति।

10. तदा व्याधः स्वर्गमगच्छत्।

11. कृष्णसूतस्तत्रागच्छत्।

12. सूतः कृष्णायानमत्।

13. कृष्णस्तमवददिदानीं लोकाद्गच्छामि।

14. संतुष्टो भव।

15. धर्मं कुरु।

16. ज्ञानं लभस्वेति॥

अभीत॰ (mfn)	fearless	सूतः (m)	charioteer
स्वर्गः (m)	heaven	लभस्व	find! *(imperative)*

CHAPTER TWENTY-FOUR

24.1 Epic Civilisation: Liberation

The final aim of all the epic literature is liberation — that is, freedom from all types of bondage, misery and ignorance. The Mahābhārata makes it clear that Yudhiṣṭhira's determination not to give up Dharma (duty), represented by a dog, prepares the way for him to be liberated in the end. The dog disappears, Yudhiṣṭhira experiences in hell the results of his misdeeds, then enjoys the bliss of complete freedom. Study of the Mahābhārata, it is said, also leads to complete freedom.

Yudhiṣṭhira refuses to give up Dharma in the form of his dog.

24.2 *Sandhi* Revision

EXERCISE 183

Write the correct vowel or consonant *sandhi* for each of the following pairs of words:

1. अभवत् हि   ....

2. अधावम् न   ....

3. एतत् लोकः   ....

4. अपिबत् शीघ्रम्   ....

5. तम् हि   ....

6. अशृणोत् नाम   ....

7. तत् खगः   ....

8. नगरात् जनः   ....

9. सीताम् इति   ....

10. एतत् भयम्   ....

11. नदीम् हि   ....

12. रामात् वनम्   ....

13. अपिबन् जलम्   ....

14. गुरु उत्तमः   ....

15. अथ इति   ....

16. कृष्ण ऋषिः   ....

17. तदा इव   ....

18. महा ऋषिः   ....

19. बहु ऐच्छत्   ....

20. नारी आसीत्   ....

21. यथा उक्तम्   ....

22. भवति इति   ....

23. देहे अतीव   ....

24. समीपे अरुणे   ....

25. शृणोति उत्तिष्ठति   ....

26. गुरो अद्य   ....

27. युद्धे अधावन्   ....

28. रात्रौ अन्या   ....

29. एव इति   ....

30. बहु एव   ....

EXERCISE 184

Give the *viyoga* forms of the following pairs of words which have been joined using vowel or consonant *sandhi:*

1. अग्नावुपविशति   ....

2. भार्यामासीत्   ....

3. त्वस्ति   ....

4. भवत्यागच्छति   ....

5. सीताया रहि   ....

6. पत्न्यात्मा   ....

7. कन्यैच्छत्   ....

8. तस्या एव   ....

9. नारीदम्   ....

10. रात्राविच्छति   ....

11. नासिकेयम्   ....

12. तदैवम्   ....

13. नार्यनुगच्छति   ....

14. नायम्   ....

15. अथर्षिः   ....

16. तारकाया एव   ....

17. दुर्जनोत्तम   ....

18. ममैकः   ....

19. हरावासीत्

20. धातृषिः

21. अत्रैकः

22. त्वय

23. बहूपरि

24. बालकोऽद्य

25. गीतेच्छति

26. रामं गच्छति

27. खगांश्चरति

28. उदराञ्शान्तिः

29. अभवन्निति

30. तच्छरः

EXERCISE 185

Apply *ac* or *hal sandhi* to the following:

1. गुरू आत्मानम्   ....

2. तत् एव   ....

3. रामवत् मार्गम्   ....

4. तथा एव   ....

5. अपि इदम्   ....

6. अग्नौ अपि   ....

7. एव ऋषिः   ....

8. सुहृत् पत्नी   ....

9. वृक्षे अस्ति   ....

10. अथ इदम्   ....

11. सीतावत् लिखति   ....

12. सीतायै इयम्   ....

13. फलम् खादति   ....

14. आसन् इति   ....

15. नदी उत्तमः   ....

[continues next page]

[continued]

16. सीता उत्तमः   ....

17. आगच्छत् शय्या   ....

18. इति अस्ति   ....

19. अभवत् तदा   ....

20. अहो * आत्मना   ....

21. तान् ते   ....

22. रामे एव   ....

23. अथ अङ्गुली   ....

24. अग्ने अचरत्   ....

25. अभवत् हस्तः   ....

26. तदा अग्निः   ....

27. तदा आत्मनः   ....

28. अतुदन् लीला   ....

29. कपिम् शान्तिः   ....

30. च ऐच्छत्   ....

* Sandhi is not applied to the final vowel of अहो.

EXERCISE 186

Apply the appropriate rules of विसर्ग सन्धि to the following:

1. वीरः अस्ति   ....

2. हेतुः खगः   ....

3. खगः यः   ....

4. रामाः अधावन्   ....

5. सः मम   ....

6. भूमेः खगः   ....

7. धातुः ऋषः   ....

8. कपिः अत्र   ....

9. ऋषः अत्र   ....

10. कपिः भवति   ....

11. खगाः फलम्   ....

12. रामयोः तस्य   ....

13. ऋषः पतति   ....

14. नौकाः रथम्   ....

15. यतः सः   ....

16. गुरुः मिलति   ....

17. पतिः खगम्   ....

18. सः एव   ....

19. हस्तैः चलति   ....

20. आत्मनः अधावन्   ....

24.3 Revision of the Past Passive Participle

EXERCISE 187

Here are ten pairs of sentences — each pair containing one sentence in Sanskrit and the other in English. Translate the Sanskrit sentences into English and the English sentences into Sanskrit.

1. **(a)** नरः गतः ।   ....

   (b) The man was born.   ....

2. **(a)** कन्या दृष्टा ।   ....

   (b) The lady was seen.   ....

3. **(a)** नृपाः हताः ।   ....

   (b) The kings were conquered.   ....

4. **(a)** फलम् खादितम् ।   ....

   (b) The fruit was grabbed.   ....

5. **(a)** मित्राणि जितानि ।   ....

   (b) The friends were slain.   ....

6. **(a)** जनकः मृतः ।   ....

   (b) The mother is dead.   ....

7. **(a)** गुरू लब्धौ ।   ....

   (b) The two teachers were seen.   ....

[continues next page]

[continued]

8. (a) दूताः त्यक्ताः। ....

   (b) The sages were abandoned. ....

9. (a) नायौ श्रुतौ ....

   (b) The two ladies were seen. ....

10. (a) धनम् लब्धम् ....

    (b) An army is found. ....

24.4 Revision of -त्वा and -य Words

Remember:

— -त्वा words mean 'having done something',
  e.g. गत्वा 'having gone'.

— -य words are formed when the verb begins with a prefix. The य is added
  to the root,
  e.g. आगम्य 'having come'.

EXERCISE 188

In this exercise, translate the following short phrases relating to -त्वा / -य words:

1. (a) दुर्जनम् दृष्ट्वा

   ....

   (b) having seen the person

   ....

2. (a) व्याघ्रम् हत्वा

   ....

   (b) having killed the snake

   ....

3. (a) जननीम् गत्वा

   ....

   (b) having gone to the teacher

   ....

4. (a) कपिम् श्रुत्वा

   ....

   (b) having heard the dog

   ....

5. (a) राजगृहम् गत्वा

   ....

   (b) having gone to the town

   ....

6. (a) राजगृहम् अश्वेन गत्वा

   ....

   (b) having gone to the town by chariot

   ....

7. (a) राजगृहम् अश्वेन गत्वा नारी दूतम् अपश्यत् ।

   ....

   (b) Having gone to the town by chariot, the man saw the king.

   ....

[continues next page]

8. (a) तृणम् अश्वाय दत्त्वा कन्या अहसत्।

....

(b) Having given the fruit to the man, the sage laughed.

....

9. (a) नारीम् आगम्य

....

(b) having come to the town

....

10. (a) नगरम् प्रविश्य

....

(b) having entered the house

....

24.5 Vocabulary for Story 24

NOUNS

अचलः (m)	mountain	द्वारम् (n)	door
भूमिः (f)	earth, ground	पितृ (m)	father
कुक्कुरः (m)	dog	धर्मः (m)	righteousness, justice
स्वर्गः (m)	heaven	भ्रातृ (m)	brother

ADJECTIVES

प्रिय°   dear

श्रुत°   heard

प्रथम°   first

समाप्त°   finished

उक्त°   spoken

द्वितीय°   second

PRONOUNS

तव   your

अहम्   I

सर्व°   all

INDECLINABLES

अन्ते	in the end	सह	together with (+ 3rd case)
आत्मनः	his own / her own	तदा	then

DHĀTUS

गम्   in going

पत्   in falling

त्यज्   in leaving

वद्   in speaking

दृश्   in seeing

VERBS

गच्छति   he goes

पतति   he falls

त्यजति   he leaves

वदति   he speaks

पश्यति   he sees

'-त्वा' ENDINGS

गत्वा   having gone

पतित्वा   having fallen

त्यक्त्वा   having left

उदित्वा   having spoken

दृष्ट्वा   having seen

24.6 Story 24

THE PĀṆḌAVAS ASCEND TO HEAVEN

The Pāṇḍavas, along with Draupadī, go off into the mountains. They all fall down dead, except Yudhiṣṭhira, who continues, followed by a dog. Yudhiṣṭhira is offered entry to heaven but is told that the dog cannot come with him. Yudhiṣṭhira refuses to go without the dog, and is told that he has passed his first test. The dog was Dharma, Yudhiṣṭhira's father. Yudhiṣṭhira is now taken to heaven, where he sees the evil Duryodhana. Yudhiṣṭhira then sees his brothers and Draupadī in hell, and insists on going to hell with them. Yudhiṣṭhira has passed his second test, of loyalty, and, along with his brothers and Draupadī, now goes to heaven and is liberated.

1. अन्ते द्रौपदी पाण्डवाश्चाचलानगच्छन् ।

2. द्रौपदीनकुलमहदेवार्जुनभीमा भूमावपतन् ।

3. युधिष्ठिरस्त्वात्मनः प्रियकुक्कुरेण सह स्वर्गद्वारमागच्छत् ।

4. तदा युधिष्ठिरेण स्वरः श्रुतः प्रियकुक्कुरमस्मिँल्लोके त्यजेति ।

5. युधिष्ठिरस्त्वात्मनः कुक्कुरं लोके नात्यजत् ।

[continues on p. 139]

The god Dharma declares Yudhiṣṭhira worthy of heaven.

[continued from p. 137]

6. स्वरोऽवदत्म* कुक्कुरस्तव पिता धर्मो नाम।

7. तव प्रथमपरीक्षा समाप्तेति।

8. तदा युधिष्ठिरो दुर्योधनं स्वर्गेऽपश्यदात्मनो भ्रातॄन्द्रौपदीं च नरकलोकेऽपश्यच्च।

9. अहमपि नरकलोकं गमिष्यामीति युधिष्ठिर उक्तवान्।

10. स्वरोऽवदत्तव द्वितीयपरीक्षा समाप्तेति।

11. तदा सर्वे पाण्डवाः स्वर्गमगच्छन्सर्वे कौरवा नरकलोकमगच्छंश्च॥

परीक्षा (f) test

* Note that सः always loses its विसर्ग except before short अ. So स कुक्कुरः, स मुनिः, but सोऽचलः.

APPENDICES

APPENDIX 1

Transliteration

The word 'Transliteration' here means the writing of Sanskrit using English letters. This Appendix shows all the Sanskrit devanāgarī letters together with the English letters used to represent them.

1. VOWELS

अ	आ	इ	ई	उ	ऊ	ऋ	ॠ	ए	ऐ	ओ	औ
a	ā	i	ī	u	ū	ṛ	ṝ	e	ai	o	au
क	का	कि	की	कु	कू	कृ	कॄ	के	कै	को	कौ
ka	kā	ki	kī	ku	kū	kṛ	kṝ	ke	kai	ko	kau

2. CONSONANTS

क	ka	च	ca	ट	ṭa	त	ta	प	pa
ख	kha	छ	cha	ठ	ṭha	थ	tha	फ	pha
ग	ga	ज	ja	ड	ḍa	द	da	ब	ba
घ	gha	झ	jha	ढ	ḍha	ध	dha	भ	bha
ङ	ṅa	ञ	ña	ण	ṇa	न	na	म	ma
ह	ha	य	ya	र	ra	ल	la	व	va
		श	śa	ष	ṣa	स	sa		

:	ḥ	◌ं	ṃ

3. HALANTA CONSONANTS

For halanta letters, the 'a' of the letter is dropped. Examples:

क् k	म् m	ट् ṭ	घ् gh	श् ś

4. JOINED CONSONANTS

(a) Standard Examples

स्य sya	ग्न gna	न्त nta	ल्प lpa	ष्प ṣpa

(b) Double-decker Examples

क्क kka	द्व dva	ङ्ग ṅga

(c) Examples of Consonants Joined with र

त्र tra	प्र pra	क्र kra	ग्र gra	ब्र bra
र्त rta	र्प rpa	र्क rka	र्ग rga	र्ब rba

(d) Some Exceptional Joined Consonants

क्ष kṣa	श्र śra	ज्ञ jña	क्त kta	ह्र hra

APPENDIX 2

Paradigms

A paradigm is an example of all the forms and endings of a word set out as a list or chart, and which is often used as a pattern for other words of a similar kind. All the paradigms used in these volumes, as well as those of the earlier Sanskrit textbooks in this series, are included in this Appendix for easy reference.

VERBS

भवति — Present Tense:

Singular	Dual	Plural
भवति he, she, it becomes	भवतः they two become	भवन्ति they become
भवसि you become	भवथः you two become	भवथ you become
भवामि I become	भवावः we two become	भवामः we become

भवति — Future Tense:

Singular	Dual	Plural
भविष्यति he, she, it will become	भविष्यतः they two will become	भविष्यन्ति they will become
भविष्यसि you will become	भविष्यथः you two will become	भविष्यथ you will become
भविष्यामि I shall become	भविष्यावः we two shall become	भविष्यामः we shall become

भवति — Past Tense:

Singular	Dual	Plural
अभवत् he, she, it became	अभवताम् they two became	अभवन् they became
अभवः you became	अभवतम् you two became	अभवत you became
अभवम् I became	अभवाव we two became	अभवाम we became

वर्धते — Present Tense:

Singular	Dual	Plural
वर्धते he, she, it grows	वर्धेते they two grow	वर्धन्ते they grow
वर्धसे you grow	वर्धेथे you two grow	वर्धध्वे you grow
वर्धे I grow	वर्धावहे we two grow	वर्धामहे we grow

वर्धते — Future Tense:

Singular	Dual	Plural
वर्धिष्यते he, she, it will grow	वर्धिष्येते they two will grow	वर्धिष्यन्ते they will grow
वर्धिष्यसे you will grow	वर्धिष्येथे you two will grow	वर्धिष्यध्वे you will grow
वर्धिष्ये I shall grow	वर्धिष्यावहे we two shall grow	वर्धिष्यामहे we shall grow

144

वर्धते — Past Tense:

Singular	Dual	Plural
अवर्धत he, she, it grew	अवर्धेताम् they two grew	अवर्धन्त they grew
अवर्धथाः you grew	अवर्धेयाम् you two grew	अवर्धध्वम् you grew
अवर्धे I grew	अवर्धावहि we two grew	अवर्धामहि we grew

लभते — Future Tense:

Singular	Dual	Plural
लप्स्यते he, she, it will find	लप्स्येते they two will find	लप्स्यन्ते they will find
लप्स्यमे you will find	लप्स्येथे you two will find	लप्स्यध्वे you will find
लप्स्ये I shall find	लप्स्यावहे we two shall find	लप्स्यामहे we shall find

खादति — Present Tense Passive:

Singular	Dual	Plural
खाद्यते he, she, it is eaten	खाद्येते they two are eaten	खाद्यन्ते they are eaten
खाद्यसे you are eaten	खाद्येथे you two are eaten	खाद्यध्वे you are eaten
खाद्ये I am eaten	खाद्यावहे we two are eaten	खाद्यामहे we are eaten

अस्ति — Present Tense:

Singular	Dual	Plural
अस्ति he, she, it is	स्तः they two are	सन्ति they are
असि you are	स्थः you two are	स्थ you are
अस्मि I am	स्वः we two are	स्मः we are

अस्ति — Past Tense:

Singular	Dual	Plural
आसीत् he, she, it was	आस्ताम् they two were	आसन् they were
आसीः you were	आस्तम् you two were	आस्त you were
आसम् I was	आस्व we two were	आस्म we were

करोति — Present Tense:

Singular	Dual	Plural
करोति he, she, it does	कुरुतः they two do	कुर्वन्ति they do
करोषि you do	कुरुथः you two do	कुरुथ you do
करोमि I do	कुर्वः we two do	कुर्मः we do

146

करोति — Future Tense:

Singular	Dual	Plural
करिष्यति he, she, it will do	करिष्यतः they two will do	करिष्यन्ति they will do
करिष्यसि you will do	करिष्यथः you two will do	करिष्यथ you will do
करिष्यामि I shall do	करिष्यावः we two shall do	करिष्यामः we shall do

करोति — Past Tense:

Singular	Dual	Plural
अकरोत् he, she, it did	अकुरुताम् they two did	अकुर्वन् they did
अकरोः you did	अकुरुतम् you two did	अकुरुत you did
अकरवम् I did	अकुर्व we two did	अकुर्म we did

For nouns, see next page.

NOUNS

रामः (Rāma): paradigm for masculine nouns ending in -अ

Singular	Dual	Plural
रामः Rāma	रामौ two Rāmas	रामाः Rāmas
हे राम O Rāma	हे रामौ O two Rāmas	हे रामाः O Rāmas
रामम् Rāma (2nd)	रामौ two Rāmas (2nd)	रामान् Rāmas (2nd)
रामेण by Rāma	रामाभ्याम् by two Rāmas	रामैः by Rāmas
रामाय for Rāma	रामाभ्याम् for two Rāmas	रामेभ्यः for Rāmas
रामात् from Rāma	रामाभ्याम् from two Rāmas	रामेभ्यः from Rāmas
रामस्य of Rāma	रामयोः of two Rāmas	रामाणाम् of Rāmas
रामे in Rāma	रामयोः in two Rāmas	रामेषु in Rāmas

मित्रम् ('friend'): paradigm for neuter nouns ending in – अम्

Singular	Dual	Plural
मित्रम् friend	मित्रे two friends	मित्राणि friends
हे मित्र O friend	हे मित्रे O two friends	हे मित्राणि O friends
मित्रम् friend (2nd)	मित्रे two friends (2nd)	मित्राणि friends (2nd)
मित्रेण by a friend	मित्राभ्याम् by two friends	मित्रैः by friends
मित्राय for a friend	मित्राभ्याम् for two friends	मित्रेभ्यः for friends
मित्रात् from a friend	मित्राभ्याम् from two friends	मित्रेभ्यः from friends
मित्रस्य of a friend	मित्रयोः of two friends	मित्राणाम् of friends
मित्रे in a friend	मित्रयोः in two friends	मित्रेषु in friends

सीता (Sītā): paradigm for feminine nouns ending in -आ

Singular	Dual	Plural
सीता Sītā	सीते two Sītās	सीताः Sītās
हे सीते O Sītā	हे सीते O two Sītās	हे सीताः O Sītās
सीताम् Sītā (2nd)	सीते two Sītās (2nd)	सीताः Sītās (2nd)
सीतया by Sītā	सीताभ्याम् by two Sītās	सीताभिः by Sītās
सीतायै for Sītā	सीताभ्याम् for two Sītās	सीताभ्यः for Sītās
सीतायाः from Sītā	सीताभ्याम् from two Sītās	सीताभ्यः from Sītās
सीतायाः of Sītā	सीतयोः of two Sītās	सीतानाम् of Sītās
सीतायाम् in Sītā	सीतयोः in two Sītās	सीतासु in Sītās

150

नदी ('river'): paradigm for feminine nouns ending in –ई

Singular	Dual	Plural
नदी river	नद्यौ two rivers	नद्यः rivers
हे नदि O river	हे नद्यौ O two rivers	हे नद्यः O rivers
नदीम् river (2nd)	नद्यौ two rivers (2nd)	नदीः rivers (2nd)
नद्या by a river	नदीभ्याम् by two rivers	नदीभिः by rivers
नद्यै for a river	नदीभ्याम् for two rivers	नदीभ्यः for rivers
नद्याः from a river	नदीभ्याम् from two rivers	नदीभ्यः from rivers
नद्याः of a river	नद्योः of two rivers	नदीनाम् of rivers
नद्याम् in a river	नद्योः in two rivers	नदीषु in rivers

हरिः ('Lord'): paradigm for masculine nouns ending in –इ

Singular	Dual	Plural
हरिः Lord	हरी two Lords	हरयः Lords
हे हरे O Lord	हे हरी O two Lords	हे हरयः O Lords
हरिम् Lord (2nd)	हरी two Lords (2nd)	हरीन् Lords (2nd)
हरिणा by the Lord	हरिभ्याम् by two Lords	हरिभिः by Lords
हरये for the Lord	हरिभ्याम् for two Lords	हरिभ्यः for Lords
हरेः from the Lord	हरिभ्याम् from two Lords	हरिभ्यः from Lords
हरेः of the Lord	हर्योः of two Lords	हरीणाम् of Lords
हरौ in the Lord	हर्योः in two Lords	हरिषु in Lords

गुरुः ('teacher'): paradigm for masculine nouns ending in – उ

Singular	Dual	Plural
गुरुः teacher	गुरू two teachers	गुरवः teachers
हे गुरो O teacher	हे गुरू O two teachers	हे गुरवः O teachers
गुरुम् teacher (2nd)	गुरू two teachers (2nd)	गुरून् teachers (2nd)
गुरुणा by the teacher	गुरुभ्याम् by two teachers	गुरुभिः by teachers
गुरवे for the teacher	गुरुभ्याम् for two teachers	गुरुभ्यः for teachers
गुरोः from the teacher	गुरुभ्याम् from two teachers	गुरुभ्यः from teachers
गुरोः of the teacher	गुर्वोः of two teachers	गुरुणाम् of teachers
गुरौ in the teacher	गुर्वोः in two teachers	गुरुषु in teachers

धातृ ('creator'): paradigm for masculine agent nouns ending in – ऋ

Singular	Dual	Plural
धाता creator	धातारौ two creators	धातारः creators
हे धातः O creator	हे धातारौ O two creators	हे धातारः O creators
धातारम् creator	धातारौ two creators (2nd)	धातॄन् creators
धात्रा by a creator	धातृभ्याम् by two creators	धातृभिः by creators
धात्रे for a creator	धातृभ्याम् for two creators	धातृभ्यः for creators
धातुः from a creator	धातृभ्याम् from two creators	धातृभ्यः from creators
धातुः of a creator	धात्रोः of two creators	धातॄणाम् of creators
धातरि in a creator	धात्रोः in two creators	धातृषु in creators

पितृ ('father'): paradigm for many masculine relationship nouns ending in – ऋ

Singular	Dual	Plural
पिता father	पितरौ two fathers	पितरः fathers
हे पितर् O father	हे पितरौ O two fathers	हे पितरः O fathers
पितरम् father	पितरौ two fathers (2nd)	पितॄन् fathers
पित्रा by a father	पितृभ्याम् by two fathers	पितृभिः by fathers
पित्रे for a father	पितृभ्याम् for two fathers	पितृभ्यः for fathers
पितुः from a father	पितृभ्याम् from two fathers	पितृभ्यः from fathers
पितुः of a father	पित्रोः of two fathers	पितॄणाम् of fathers
पितरि in a father	पित्रोः in two fathers	पितृषु in fathers

मातृ ('mother'): paradigm for many feminine relationship nouns ending in – ऋ

Singular	Dual	Plural
माता mother	मातरौ two mothers	मातरः mothers
हे मातर् O mother	हे मातरौ O two mothers	हे मातरः O mothers
मातरम् mother	मातरौ two mothers (2nd)	मातॄः mothers
मात्रा by a mother	मातृभ्याम् by two mothers	मातृभिः by mothers
मात्रे for a mother	मातृभ्याम् for two mothers	मातृभ्यः for mothers
मातुः from a mother	मातृभ्याम् from two mothers	मातृभ्यः from mothers
मातुः of a mother	मात्रोः of two mothers	मातॄणाम् of mothers
मातरि in a mother	मात्रोः in two mothers	मातृषु in mothers

राजन् ('king'): paradigm for masculine words ending in -**अन्**

	Singular	*Dual*	*Plural*
1st	राजा	राजानौ	राजानः
Voc.	हे राजन्	हे राजानौ	हे राजानः
2nd	राजानम्	राजानौ	राज्ञः
3rd	राज्ञा	राजभ्याम्	राजभिः
4th	राज्ञे	राजभ्याम्	राजभ्यः
5th	राज्ञः	राजभ्याम्	राजभ्यः
6th	राज्ञः	राज्ञोः	राज्ञाम्
7th	राज्ञि	राज्ञोः	राजसु

आत्मन् ('Self'): paradigm for masculine words ending in -**अन्** containing a conjunct consonant.

	Singular	*Dual*	*Plural*
1st	आत्मा	आत्मानौ	आत्मानः
Voc.	हे आत्मन्	हे आत्मानौ	हे आत्मानः
2nd	आत्मानम्	आत्मानौ	आत्मनः
3rd	आत्मना	आत्मभ्याम्	आत्मभिः
4th	आत्मने	आत्मभ्याम्	आत्मभ्यः
5th	आत्मनः	आत्मभ्याम्	आत्मभ्यः
6th	आत्मनः	आत्मनोः	आत्मनाम्
7th	आत्मनि	आत्मनोः	आत्मसु

नामन् ('name'): paradigm for neuter words ending in -अन्

	Singular	Dual	Plural
1st	नाम	नाम्नी/नामनी	नामानि
Voc.	हे नामन्/नाम	हे नाम्नी/नामनी	हे नामानि
2nd	नाम	नाम्नी/नामनी	नामानि
3rd	नाम्ना	नामभ्याम्	नामभिः
4th	नाम्ने	नामभ्याम्	नामभ्यः
5th	नाम्नः	नामभ्याम्	नामभ्यः
6th	नाम्नः	नाम्नोः	नाम्नाम्
7th	नाम्नि/नामनि	नाम्नोः	नामसु

कर्मन् ('action'): paradigm for neuter words ending in -अन् containing a conjunct consonant

	Singular	Dual	Plural
1st	कर्म	कर्मणी	कर्माणि
Voc.	हे कर्म	हे कर्मणी	हे कर्माणि
2nd	कर्म	कर्मणी	कर्माणि
3rd	कर्मणा	कर्मभ्याम्	कर्मभिः
4th	कर्मणे	कर्मभ्याम्	कर्मभ्यः
5th	कर्मणः	कर्मभ्याम्	कर्मभ्यः
6th	कर्मणः	कर्मणोः	कर्मणाम्
7th	कर्मणि	कर्मणोः	कर्मसु

मनस् ('mind'): paradigm for neuter words ending in -अस्

	Singular	Dual	Plural
1st	मनः	मनसी	मनांसि
Voc.	हे मनः	हे मनसी	हे मनांसि
2nd	मनः	मनसी	मनांसि
3rd	मनसा	मनोभ्याम्	मनोभिः
4th	मनसे	मनोभ्याम्	मनोभ्यः
5th	मनसः	मनोभ्याम्	मनोभ्यः
6th	मनसः	मनसोः	मनसाम्
7th	मनसि	मनसोः	मनःसु

ज्ञानिन् ('wise one'): paradigm for masculine words ending in -इन्

	Singular	Dual	Plural
1st	ज्ञानी	ज्ञानिनौ	ज्ञानिनः
Voc.	हे ज्ञानिन्	हे ज्ञानिनौ	हे ज्ञानिनः
2nd	ज्ञानिनम्	ज्ञानिनौ	ज्ञानिनः
3rd	ज्ञानिना	ज्ञानिभ्याम्	ज्ञानिभिः
4th	ज्ञानिने	ज्ञानिभ्याम्	ज्ञानिभ्यः
5th	ज्ञानिनः	ज्ञानिभ्याम्	ज्ञानिभ्यः
6th	ज्ञानिनः	ज्ञानिनोः	ज्ञानिनाम्
7th	ज्ञानिनि	ज्ञानिनोः	ज्ञानिषु

ज्ञानिनी ('wise'): paradigm for feminine words ending in -इन्

	Singular	Dual	Plural
1st	ज्ञानिनी	ज्ञानिन्यौ	ज्ञानिन्यः
Voc.	हे ज्ञानिनि	हे ज्ञानिन्यौ	हे ज्ञानिन्यः
2nd	ज्ञानिनीम्	ज्ञानिन्यौ	ज्ञानिनीः
3rd	ज्ञानिन्या	ज्ञानिनीभ्याम्	ज्ञानिनीभिः
4th	ज्ञानिन्यै	ज्ञानिनीभ्याम्	ज्ञानिनीभ्यः
5th	ज्ञानिन्याः	ज्ञानिनीभ्याम्	ज्ञानिनीभ्यः
6th	ज्ञानिन्याः	ज्ञानिन्योः	ज्ञानिनीनाम्
7th	ज्ञानिन्याम्	ज्ञानिन्योः	ज्ञानिनीषु

धीमत् ('possessing wisdom'): paradigm for masculine words ending in -मत् or -वत्

	Singular	Dual	Plural
1st	धीमान्	धीमन्तौ	धीमन्तः
Voc.	हे धीमन्	हे धीमन्तौ	हे धीमन्तः
2nd	धीमन्तम्	धीमन्तौ	धीमतः
3rd	धीमता	धीमद्भ्याम्	धीमद्भिः
4th	धीमते	धीमद्भ्याम्	धीमद्भ्यः
5th	धीमतः	धीमद्भ्याम्	धीमद्भ्यः
6th	धीमतः	धीमतोः	धीमताम्
7th	धीमति	धीमतोः	धीमत्सु

धीमती ('possessing wisdom'): paradigm for feminine words ending in - मत् or - वत्

	Singular	Dual	Plural
1st	धीमती	धीमत्यौ	धीमत्यः
Voc.	हे धीमति	हे धीमत्यौ	हे धीमत्यः
2nd	धीमतीम्	धीमत्यौ	धीमतीः
3rd	धीमत्या	धीमतीभ्याम्	धीमतीभिः
4th	धीमत्यै	धीमतीभ्याम्	धीमतीभ्यः
5th	धीमत्याः	धीमतीभ्याम्	धीमतीभ्यः
6th	धीमत्याः	धीमत्योः	धीमतीनाम्
7th	धीमत्याम्	धीमत्योः	धीमतीषु

मतिः ('thought'): paradigm for feminine words ending in - इ

	Singular	Dual	Plural
1st	मतिः	मती	मतयः
Voc.	हे मते	हे मती	हे मतयः
2nd	मतिम्	मती	मतीः
3rd	मत्या	मतिभ्याम्	मतिभिः
4th	मतये	मतिभ्याम्	मतिभ्यः
5th	मतेः	मतिभ्याम्	मतिभ्यः
6th	मतेः	मत्योः	मतीनाम्
7th	मतौ/मत्याम्	मत्योः	मतिषु

For pronouns, see next page.

PRONOUNS

तत् ('that'): paradigm for the *neuter* forms of this pronoun

Singular	Dual	Plural
तत् that	ते those two	तानि those
तत् that (2nd)	ते those two (2nd)	तानि those (2nd)
तेन by that	ताभ्याम् by those two	तैः by those
तस्मै for that	ताभ्याम् for those two	तेभ्यः for those
तस्मात् from that	ताभ्याम् from those two	तेभ्यः from those
तस्य of that	तयोः of those two	तेषाम् of those
तस्मिन् in that	तयोः in those two	तेषु in those

Note: In the dual and plural, 2nd case onwards,
sometimes तत् *is translated as 'them'.*

162

तत् ('he / that'): paradigm for the *masculine* forms of this pronoun

Singular	Dual	Plural
सः he, that	तौ those two	ते those
तम् him, that (2nd)	तौ those two (2nd)	तान् those (2nd)
तेन by him, by that	ताभ्याम् by those two	तैः by those
तस्मै for him, for that	ताभ्याम् for those two	तेभ्यः for those
तस्मात् from him, from that	ताभ्याम् from those two	तेभ्यः from those
तस्य of him, of that	तयोः of those two	तेषाम् of those
तस्मिन् in him, in that	तयोः in those two	तेषु in those

Note: In the dual and plural, 2nd Ending onwards,
sometimes तत् is translated as 'them'.

तत् ('she / that'): paradigm for the *feminine* forms of this pronoun

Singular	Dual	Plural
सा she, that	ते those two	ताः those
ताम् her, that (2nd)	ते those two (2nd)	ताः those (2nd)
तया by her, by that	ताभ्याम् by those two	ताभिः by those
तस्यै for her, for that	ताभ्याम् for those two	ताभ्यः for those
तस्याः from her, from that	ताभ्याम् from those two	ताभ्यः from those
तस्याः of her, of that	तयोः of those two	तासाम् of those
तस्याम् in her, in that	तयोः in those two	तासु in those

*Note: In the dual and plural, 2nd Ending onwards,
sometimes* तत् *is translated as 'them'.*

किम् ('what? / which?'): paradigm for the *neuter* forms of this pronoun

Singular	Dual	Plural
किम् what? / which?	के which two?	कानि which?
किम् to what? / to which? (2nd)	के to which two? (2nd)	कानि to which? (2nd)
केन by what? / by which?	काभ्याम् by which two?	कैः by which?
कस्मै for what? / for which?	काभ्याम् for which two?	केभ्यः for which?
कस्मात् from what?/from which?	काभ्याम् from which two?	केभ्यः from which?
कस्य of what? / of which?	कयोः of which two?	केषाम् of which?
कस्मिन् in what? / in which?	कयोः in which two?	केषु in which?

कः ('who? / which?'): paradigm of the *masculine* forms of this pronoun

Singular	Dual	Plural
कः who? / which?	कौ which two?	के which?
कम् to whom? / to which?	कौ to which two? (2nd)	कान् to which? (2nd)
केन by whom? / by which?	काभ्याम् by which two?	कैः by which?
कस्मै for whom? / for which?	काभ्याम् for which two?	केभ्यः for which?
कस्मात् from whom? / from which?	काभ्याम् from which two?	केभ्यः from which?
कस्य of whom? / of which?	कयोः of which two?	केषाम् of which?
कस्मिन् in whom? / in which?	कयोः in which two?	केषु in which?

का ('who? / which?'): paradigm of the *feminine* forms of this pronoun

Singular	Dual	Plural
का who? / which?	के which two?	काः which?
काम् to whom? / to which? (2nd)	के to which two? (2nd)	काः to which? (2nd)
कया by whom? / by which?	काभ्याम् by which two?	काभिः by which?
कस्यै for whom? / for which?	काभ्याम् for which two?	काभ्यः for which?
कस्याः from whom?/ from which?	काभ्याम् from which two?	काभ्यः from which?
कस्याः of whom? / of which?	कयोः of which two?	कासाम् of which?
कस्याम् in whom? / in which?	कयोः in which two?	कासु in which?

The paradigm of अहम् ('I'):

Singular	Dual	Plural
अहम् I	आवाम् we two	वयम् we
माम् me (2nd)	आवाम् us two (2nd)	अस्मान् us (2nd)
मया by me	आवाभ्याम् by us two	अस्माभिः by us
मह्यम् for me	आवाभ्याम् for us two	अस्मभ्यम् for us
मत् from me	आवाभ्याम् from us two	अस्मत् from us
मम of me	आवयोः of us two	अस्माकम् of us
मयि in me	आवयोः in us two	अस्मासु in us

The paradigm of त्वम् ('you'):

Singular	Dual	Plural
त्वम् you	युवाम् you two	यूयम् you
त्वाम् you (2nd)	युवाम् you two (2nd)	युष्मान् you (2nd)
त्वया by you	युवाभ्याम् by you two	युष्माभिः by you
तुभ्यम् for you	युवाभ्याम् for you two	युष्मभ्यम् for you
त्वत् from you	युवाभ्याम् from you two	युष्मत् from you
तव of you	युवयोः of you two	युष्माकम् of you
त्वयि in you	युवयोः in you two	युष्मासु in you

APPENDIX 3

Vocabulary: English – Sanskrit

This English–Sanskrit vocabulary comprises in alphabetical order the appropriate English renderings of all the Sanskrit words used in the exercises and stories found in Parts 1, 2 and 3 of this book, as well as those used in the earlier Sanskrit textbooks, 'The Stories of Krishna' and 'The Story of Rāma'.

A

abandoned	त्यक्त॰
(he/she/it) abandoned	अत्यजत
(is) able	शक्नोति
able, skilled	कुशल॰
action	कर्मन्
afraid	भीत॰
again	पुनः
again and again	पुनः पुनः
Agha, name of a demon	अघः
alas! alas!	हा हा
(sets) alight	दाहयति
all, everything	सर्व॰
alone, only	एव
	(emphasises previous word)
also, even	अपि
amazed	विस्मित॰
amazement, astonishment	विस्मयः

Ambālika	अम्बालिका
Ambā	अम्बा
Ambika	अम्बिका
anointing, coronation, sprinkling	अभिषेकः
and	च
angry	कुपित॰
another	अन्य॰
answers, replies	प्रतिवदति
any (one), some (one), a certain	किं चित्
aphrorism, rule; thread rope, string	सूत्रम्
approaches	उपगच्छति
are – they (plural) are	सन्ति
– they two are	स्तः
– we (plural) are	स्मः
– we two are	स्वः
– you (sing.) are	असि
– you (plural) are	स्थ
– you two are	स्थः
(having) arisen	उद्भूय
arises	उद्भवति

Arjuna	अर्जुनः	beautiful	रमणीय°, रुचिर°,
arm	बाहुः (m)		सुन्दरः (m), सुन्दरी (f)
army	सेना	(having a) beautiful form,	
around	अभितः	handsome	रूपवत्
arrow	शरः		सुन्दर°/ -री°
as if, like	इव	became	अभवत, भूतवत्
asked	अपृच्छत्	be!, become!	भव (sg.), भवत (pl.)
(having) asked	पृष्ट्वा	(having) become	भूत्वा
asks	पृच्छति	(let him/her/it) become	भवतु
asks for	प्रार्थयति	(will) become	भविष्यति
Aśoka trees	अशोकवृक्षाः	becomes	भवति
astonishment, amazement	विस्मयः	before	पूर्वम् (+ 5th)
ate	अखादत्, खादितवत्°	belly	उदरः
attacks	अभिधावति	beneath	अधः (+ 6th)
attendant, servant	सेवकः	best	उत्तम°, श्रेष्ठ°
austerity	तपस्	Bharata	भरतः
awake	बुद्ध°	Bhīma	भीमः
Ayodhyā	अयोध्या	Bhīṣma	भीष्मः
		binds	बध्नाति
		bird	खगः, पक्षिन् (m), पक्षिनी (f)
B		bitten	दष्ट°
		black	कृष्ण°
		blessed, lord	भगवत्
bad omen	दुर्मङ्गलम्	blind	अन्ध°
bad person	दुर्जनः	bliss	आनन्दः
ball	मण्डलम्	blood	रक्तम्
bank (of a river)	तीरम्	blue	नील°
battle	युद्धम्	boat	नौका
does battle	युद्धम् करोति	body	देहः
		book	पुस्तकम्

born	जात॰		
(having) bound	बद्ध्वा		
bow [the noun]	चापः		
(a) bow, homage	नमस्		
bowed	अनमत्	**C**	
(having) bowed	नत्वा		
bows [the verb]	नमति	calf	वत्सः
boy	बालकः	came	आगच्छत्, आगतवत्
Brahmā weapon	ब्रह्मास्त्रम्	cat	बिडालः
brave	वीर॰	Cāṇūra	चाणूरः
breakfast	प्रातराशः	carried off	अपहृत॰
breaks, splits, destroys	भेदयति	cattle	पशवः (pl. of पशुः)
breast	स्तनः	causeway	सेतुः
bring near, place before	उपहरति	cave	गुहा
bring!	आनय	chair	पीठम्
brings	आनयति	chariot	रथः
broken	भिन्न॰	charioteer	सूतः
brother	सोदरः, भ्रातृ	cheating; sin	अधर्मः
brought	आनयत्	chin	चिबुकम्
built	अकरोत्	chosen	वृत॰
(it was) built, made	अक्रियत	city, town	नगरम्
bull	ऋषभः	climbs	आरोहति
(will) burn	धक्ष्यति	climbs down	अवरोहति
burned	अदहत्	closes (the eyes)	निमिषति
burns	दहति	(having) closed the eyes	निमिष्य
burnt	दग्ध॰	cloud	मेघः
(having) burnt	दग्ध्वा	club, mace	गदा
but	तु	colour	वर्णः
butter	नवनीतम्	come	आगत॰
		come! (sing.)	आगच्छ
		come! (pl.)	आगच्छत
		(having) come	आगम्य

172

(let) come!	आगच्छतु		**D**
(will) come	आगमिष्यति		
come together, gather	समागच्छति		
comes	आगच्छति	dancer	नाटकः
comes back	प्रत्यागच्छति	darkness	तमस् (n.)
comes out	निर्गच्छति	Daśaratha	दशरथः
command; word	वचनम्	daughter, girl, maiden	कन्या
(will) conquer	जेष्यति	dead	मृत॰
conquered	जित॰, अजयत्	dear	प्रिय॰
conquers, is victorious	जयति	death	मरणम्
contented	संतुष्ट॰	deer, forest animal	मृगः
coronation, anointing	अभिषेकः	demon	राक्षसः
covered	आवृत॰	demoness	राक्षसी
cowherd	गोपालः	desire	कामः
counsellor, minister	मन्त्रिन् (m.)	(he/she) desires, wants	इच्छति
Creator, the	पितामहः	(they) desired, wanted	ऐच्छन्
creator	धातृ (m.)	(having) desired, wanted	इष्ट्वा
cried out	अक्रोशत्	destroyed, ruined	अनाशयत्, नष्ट॰
(having) cried out	क्रुष्ट्वा	destroys	नाशयति, भेदयति
cried; wailed	अरोदत्	Dhṛtarāṣṭra	धृतराष्ट्रः
cries out	क्रोशति	(they pl.) did, made	अकुर्वन्
cries; wails	रोदति	(he/she/it) did, made	अकरोत्
crossed	अतरत्	discipline, austerity, fire	तपस् (n.)
crosses	तरति	do! (sg.)	कुरु
crow	काकः	do! (pl.)	कुरुत
curse	शापः	(let him/her) do	करोतु
cursed	शप्त॰	(will) do, make	करिष्यति
cut	छिन्न॰	does, makes, puts on	करोति
(having) cut	छित्त्वा	dog	कुक्कुरः

done, made, put on	कृत°, कृतवत्	eldest	ज्येष्ठ°
(having) done, made, put on	कृत्वा	elephant	गजः
donkey	गर्दभः	embraced	पर्यष्वजत
door	द्वारम्	enemy	अरिः, शत्रुः (m)
drank	अपिबत्	end, inside	अन्तः
dream, sleep	स्वप्नः	(in the) end	अन्ते
drink!	पिब (sg.), पिबत (pl.)	entered	प्राविशत्
drinks	पिबति	(having) entered	प्रविश्य
Droṇa	द्रोणः	enters	प्रविशति
drunk	पीत°	entrusts	निक्षिपति
(having) drunk	पीत्वा	even, also	अपि
Duryodhana	दुर्योधनः	everything	सर्वम्
dust	रजम्	everywhere	सर्वत्र
dwells	वसति	evil	असाधु°, दुष्ट°, दुष्कृत°
dwelt	अवसत्	experienced	अनुभूत°
		experiences, feels	अनुभवति
		eye	नेत्रम्

E

ear	कर्णः
earth	पृथिवी (f.)
eat!	खाद (sg.), खादत (pl.)
(will) eat	खादिष्यति
eaten	खादित°
(was) eaten	अखाद्यत
(will be) eaten	खादिष्यते
eats	खादति
eighth	अष्टम°
Ekalavya	एकलव्यः

F

face	मुखम्
falls	पतति
(having) fallen	पतित्वा
falls in love	स्निह्यति (+7th)
far away	दूरे
farmer, trader	वैश्यः
father; Janaka	पितृ, जनकः
fault	दोषः

fear	भयम्	fruit	फलम्
fearless	अभय॰		
fell	अपतत्, पतितवत्		
fell in love	अस्निह्यत् (+7th)	**G**	
(will) find	लप्स्यते		
finds	लभते	Gaṅgā	गङ्गा
finished	समाप्त॰	Gāndhārī	गान्धारी
fire	अग्निः, तपस्	garden	उद्यानम्
(possessing) fire	अग्निमत्	gather, come together	समागच्छति
first	प्रथम॰	gave	अददात्
fish	मत्स्यः	gift	दानम्
fisherman	धीवरः	girl, daughter	कन्या
five	पञ्च॰	give!	देहि (sg.)
flower	पुष्पम्	(will) give	दास्यति
flesh, meat	मांसम्	given	दत्त॰
flute	वंशः	(having) given	दत्त्वा
follows	अनुगच्छति, अनुधावति	gives	ददाति
(is) fond of	स्निह्यति (+ 7th)	(will) give help	
food	अन्नम्		साहाय्यम् करिष्यति
(like a) fool	मूढवत्	go!	गच्छ (sg.), गच्छत (pl.)
foot	पादः	(let him/her/it) go	गच्छतु
forest	वनम्, अरण्यम्	(will) go	गमिष्यति
forgets	विस्मरति	god	देवः
form	रूपम्	goddess	देवी
found	अलभत, लब्ध॰	goes	गच्छति
(having) found	लब्ध्वा	goes away	अपगच्छति
freed	मुक्त॰ (+5th)	goes down	अवगच्छति
friend	मित्रम्	goes forward	प्रगच्छति
frightened	भीत॰	goes out	निर्गच्छति

golden	सुवर्ण॰
gone	गत॰
(having) gone	गत्वा
(it will be) gone to	गमिष्यते
good	साधु॰
good! good!	साधु साधु
(having) good fortune, blessed; lord	भगवत्
grabbed	गृहीत॰
(having) grabbed	गृहीत्वा
grass	तृणम्
great	महत्, महा- (at the beginning of a compound)
green	हरित॰
grew	अवर्धत
grief	शोकः
ground, earth	भूमिः(f.), भूमिम् (2nd)
(on the) ground	भूम्याम् (7th)
grows	वर्धते
(will) grow	वर्धिष्यते

H

hair	केशः
hall, room	शाला
hand	हस्तः
handsome	सुन्दर॰/ -री॰, रूपवत्
Hanumān, son of the wind	वायुपुत्रः
happiness, pleasure	सुखम्
happy	सुखित॰
he, that	सः
head	शिरस् (n)
healthy	कुशल॰
heard	श्रुत॰, श्रुतवत्
(having) heard	श्रुत्वा
hears, listens	शृणोति
heart	हृदयम्
heaven	स्वर्गः
heir apparent	युवराजः
help	साहाय्यम्
(will give) help	साहाय्यम् करिष्यति
her (2nd)	ताम्
(to) her (4th)	तस्यै
her, of her (6th)	तस्याः
her/his own	आत्मनः (m./f.)
here	अत्र
hidden	तिरोहित॰
him (2nd)	तम्
(by) him (3rd)	तेन
(to) him (4th)	तस्मै
his, of him (6th)	तस्य
hit	तुदित॰
hits	तुदति
hole, opening	विवरः

home	गृहम्
horrible	घोर॰
horse	अश्वः
house	गृहम्
how?	कथम्
(a) hundred	शतम्
hunter	व्याधः
husband	भर्तृ
husband, lord	पतिः

I

I	अहम्
I am	अस्मि
if	यदि
Indra	इन्द्रः
Indrajit	इन्द्रजित्
inside	अन्तः
intellect, intelligence	बुद्धिः (f.)
is, exists	अस्ति
it / that	तत्

J

Janaka	जनकः
jealousy	ईर्ष्या
jewel	मणिः (m.), भूषणम्

jump (the noun)	प्लवनम्
justice, law, righteousness	धर्मः

K

Kabandha	कबन्धः
Karṇa	कर्णः
Kaṃsa	कंसः
Kāliya, a serpent demon	कालियः
Kaurava	कौरवः
kill!	व्यापादय
(will) kill	व्यापादयिष्यति
kills	व्यापादयति
killed	हत॰, व्यापादित॰, व्यापादितवत्
(having) killed	हत्वा
king	नृपः, राजन्
kingdom	राज्यम्
Kubera, the god of wealth	कुबेरः
Kuntī	कुन्ती
Kṛṣṇa	कृष्णः
Kaikeyī	कैकेयी
Kausalyā	कौसल्या
knowledge	ज्ञानम्
known	ज्ञात॰

L

lake	सरस् (n.)
Lakṣmaṇa	लक्ष्मणः
Laṅkā, Rāvaṇa's island	लङ्का
lady	नारी
large	विशाल॰
laughed	अहसत्
(having) laughed	हसित्वा
laughs	हसति
(bursts into) laughter	प्रहसति
law, justice, righteousness	धर्मः
leads	नयति
(will) lead	नेष्यति
leaf-house	पर्णगृहम्
(having) left	त्यक्ता
leave alone!	त्यज (sg.), त्यजत (pl.)
leaves	त्यजति
led	अनयत्
(having) led	नीत्वा
(he/she/it) left, abandoned	अत्यजत्
lifted up	उदहरत्
lifts, lifts up	उद्धरति
like, as if	इव
like a fool	मूढवत्
like Rāma	रामवत्
likewise; thus	एवम्

limitless	अनन्त॰
lion	सिंहः
(let) listen	शृणोतु
listen!	शृणु (sg.), शृणुत (pl.)
listened	अशृणोत्
listens, hears	शृणोति
live!	जीव (sg.), जीवत (pl.)
lives	जीवति
(having) lived	जीवित्वा
lives, dwells	वसति
lives in, inhabits	निवसति
long	दीर्घ॰
long ago	पुरा
(for a) long time	चिरेण, बहुकालम्
Lord, the	हरिः
lord, husband	पतिः

M

mace, club	गदा
made, did, built	अकरोत्
(they pl.) made, did	अकुर्वन्
Mādrī	माद्री (f.)
magic	माया
magical snake	नागः
(will) make, do	करिष्यति
makes, does	करोति

178

(having) made, done	कृत्वा	mouth	आस्यम्, मुखम्
man	नरः	much, many	बहु॰
mantra	मन्त्रः	mud	पङ्कः
many, much	बहु॰	my [*lit.* of me]	मम
Mārīca	मारीचः		
marriage	विवाहः		
(having) married	परिणीय		
marries	परिनयति		
master	स्वामिन्		
me (2nd)	माम्	**N**	
(by) me	मया		
(for) me	मह्यम्		
(in) me	मयि	naked	नग्न॰
meat, flesh	मांसम्	Nakula	नकुलः
meets	मिलति (+ 3rd)	Nala	नलः
messenger	दूतः	name	नामन् (n.)
met	अमिलत् (+ 3rd)	name, by name	नाम
(having) met	मिलित्वा	Nārada, a sage	नारदः
(in the) middle of	मध्ये (+ 6th)	near	समीपे (+6th)
mighty, strongest	बलिष्ठ॰	neck	ग्रीवः
mind	मनस् (n)	nectar (of immortality)	अमृतम्
minister, counsellor	मन्त्रिन्	never	न कदा अपि
Mithilā	मिथिला (f.)	night	रात्रिः (f.)
monk	मुनिजनः	Nīla, (a monkey architect)	नीलः
monkey	कपिः, वानरः	nose	नासिका (f.)
moon	चन्द्रः	not	न
mother	जननी, मातृ	nothing	न किञ्चित्
mountain	अचलः	now	अधुना, इदानीम्
mouse	मूषिकः	nowhere	न कुत्रचित्

O

O!	हे
ocean	समुद्रः
old	वृद्ध॰
(a bad) omen	दुर्मङ्गलम्
O my!	अहो
once, once upon a time	एकदा
one, a certain	एक॰
only, alone (emphasises previous word)	एव
(an) opening; hole	विवरः
opens eyes	उन्मिषति
orange	नारङ्ग॰
other, another	अन्य॰
outcast	निषादः
own body	स्वदेहः
his own / her own	आत्मनः

P

palace	राजगृहम्
pale	पाण्डु॰
Pāṇḍava	पाण्डवः
Pāṇḍu	पाण्डुः
part	भागः
party	उत्सवः

peace	शान्तिः (f.)
people	जनाः
person	जनः, पुरुषः
pigeon	कपोतः
pillar	स्तम्भः
place before, bring near	उपहरति
places, puts	स्थापयति
(having) played	क्रीडित्वा
(he/she/it) played	अक्रीडत्
plays	क्रीडति
plays (an instrument)	वादयति
please	दयया
pleasure, happiness	सुखम्
poison	विषम्
possessing	युक्त॰(+3rd), –वत्॰, –मत्॰
possessing	
a beautiful form	रूपवत्॰
fire	अग्निमत्॰
good fortune	भगवत्॰
strength, power	बलवत्॰
wealth, virtue	धनिन्॰
wisdom	धीमत्॰
powerful, having strength	बलिन्॰
previously	पूर्वम्
prince	राजपुत्रः
protect!, save!	रक्ष
protects, saves	रक्षति
protected, saved	रक्षित॰
proud	गर्वित॰
punish!	दण्डय
pupil	शिष्यः

pure	शुद्ध॰	righteous, just	धार्मिक॰
Pūtanā, a demoness	पूतना	ring	अङ्गुलीयम्
puts on; does, makes	करोति	river	नदी
		road	मार्गः
		rock	शिला
		room	शाला
		rope, string; rule	सूत्रम्
		ruined, destroyed	नष्ट॰
		(having) run after	अनुधाव्य
		(let) run	धावतु

Q

queen	राज्ञी
quickly	शीघ्रम्

run!	धाव, (sg.), धावत (pl.)
runs	धावति
runs after, follows	अनुधावति
runs against/towards	अभिधावति

R

rabbit	शशकः
Rāhu (a demon)	राहुः
rains	वर्षाः
Rāma	रामः
ran	अधावत्, धावितवत्॰
Rāvaṇa	रावणः
red	अरुण॰
rejoiced	अरमत
rejoices	रमते
(having) replied	प्रत्युद्य
replies, answers	प्रतिवदति
righteousness, law, justice	धर्मः

S

sacrifices	जुहोति
sad	दुःखित॰
sage	मुनिजनः, ऋषिः, मुनिः
Sahadeva	सहदेवः
said, spoke	अवदत्, उक्तवत्॰
(having) said, spoken	उदित्वा
(he/she) said	आह
(for the)) sake of	-अर्थम्
	(at the end of a compound)
sang	अगायत्

Śatrughna	शत्रुघ्नः	silently	तूष्णीम्
Satyavatī	सत्यवती (f.)	sin; cheating	अधर्मः
saved	रक्षित॰	since ... therefore	यस्मात्...तस्मात्
saves, protects	रक्षति	sings	गायति
saw	अपश्यत्	Sītā	सीता
says, speaks	वदति	sits down	उपविशति
Śāntanu	शान्तनुः	Śiva	शिवः
searched after	अन्वैच्छत्	skilled, able	कुशल॰
second	द्वितीय॰	sky	गगनम्
see!	पश्य (sg.), पश्यत (pl.)	sleep, dream	स्वप्नः
(let) see	पश्यतु	small	अल्प॰
(will) see	द्रक्ष्यति	smell	गन्धः
seen	दृष्ट॰, दृष्टवत्	(bad) smell	दुर्गन्धः
(having) seen	दृष्ट्वा	(good) smell	सुगन्धः
(it will be) seen	द्रक्ष्यते	(with a) smile	सस्मितम्
sees	पश्यति	snake	सर्पः
self-choice ceremony	स्वयंवरः	(magical) snake	नागः
serpent demon	कालियः	soldier	सैनिकः
servant or labourer	शूद्रः, सेवकः	somebody, someone, something	
(having) set alight	दग्ध्वा	(m) कः चित् / चन / अपि	
set light to	अदाहयत्	(f) का चित् / चन / अपि	
sets light to	दाहयति,	(n) किं चित् / चन / अपि	
seven	सप्त	son	पुत्रः
she, that	सा	soon	अचिरेण
shines	भाति	sorrow	दुःखम्
shoots, throws	क्षिपति	sound, voice	शब्दः
(having) shot/thrown	क्षिप्त्वा	speak!	वद (sg.), वदत (pl.)
short	ह्रस्व॰	(let) speak	वदतु
shot	क्षिप्त॰	speaks, says	वदति

special	विशिष्ट॰
splits, breaks, destroys	भेदयति
spoken	उक्त॰
(having) spoken	उदित्वा
(thorough) sprinkling, anointing; coronation	अभिषेकः
stands	तिष्ठति
stands up	उत्तिष्ठति
star	तारका
statue	मूर्तिः (f.)
stood	अतिष्ठत्
(thorough) sprinkling, anointing; coronation	अभिषेकः
stands	तिष्ठति
stands up	उत्तिष्ठति
star	तारका
statement, word, command	वचनम्
statue	मूर्तिः (f.)
stood	अतिष्ठत्
stop!	उपरम
Sumitrā	सुमित्रा (f.)
Śūrpanakhā	शूर्पनखा (f.)
sun	सूर्यः
sunk	निमग्न॰
Supreme Lord, the	परमेश्वरः
sweetheart, friend	सुहृत् (m.)
sword	खड्गः

T

tail	पुच्छम्, पुच्छः
teacher	आचार्यः, गुरुः
test	परीक्षा (f.)
thank you	वन्दनम्
that, it	तत्
that, he	सः
that, she	सा
that, him (2nd)	तम्
that, her (2nd)	ताम्
(in) that, (in) him	तस्मिन्
then, at that time	तदा, तर्हि
there	तत्र
there is	अस्ति
therefore	तस्मात्
there was	आसीत्
they two are	स्तः
they (plural) were	आसन्
thigh	ऊरुः
thinks	चिन्तयति
(he, she) thought	अचिन्तयत्
(it will be) thought of	चिन्तयिष्यते ते
those (m. pl.)	ते
those (2nd masc. pl.)	तान्
thought	मतिः
(having) thought	चिन्तयित्वा
thread, rope; aphorism	सूत्रम्

throw down, put trust in	निक्षिपति	(by) us (plural)	अस्माभिः
(having) thrown/shot	क्षिप्त्वा	(for) us (plural)	अस्मभ्यम्
throws, shoots	क्षिपति	(from) us (plural)	अस्मत्
thumb	अङ्गुली/अङ्गुलः	(in) us (plural)	अस्मासु
'thus'	इति	(of) us (plural)	अस्माकम्
thus; likewise	एवम्	us/we two	आवाम्
tiger	व्याघ्रः	Uttarā	उत्तरा
time	कालः		
(in) time	कालेन		
together with	सह (+ 3rd)		
told	अकथ्यत्		
tormented	पीडित॰		

V

towards (used after a 2nd-case word)	प्रति	very	अतीव
town, city	नगरम्	Vicitravīrya	विचित्रवीर्यः
trader, farmer	वैश्यः	(is) victorious	जयति
tree	वृक्षः	(let be) victorious	जयतु
true	सत्य॰	virtuous; having wealth	धनिन्
(put) trust in	निक्षिपति	Viśvāmitra	विश्वामित्रः
		voice, sound	स्वरः, शब्दः
		vow	व्रतम्
		vulture	गृध्रः
		Vyāsa	व्यासः

U

W

unburnt	अदग्ध॰		
understands, goes down	अवगच्छति		
unhappily	दुःखेन	wailed, cried	अरोदत्
unhappiness	दुःखम्	wails, cries	रोदति
unlawful act	अधर्मः		
us (plural, 2nd)	अस्मान्		

walk!	चर (sg.), चरत (pl.),
(will) walk	चरिष्यति
walked	अचरत्
(having) walked	चरित्वा
(it will be) walked	चरिष्यते
walks	चरति
(they) wanted, desired	ऐच्छन्
wants, desires	इच्छति
was	
(he/she/it was; there was)	आसीत्
(I was)	आसम्
water	जलम्
we (plural)	वयम्
(having) wealth; virtuous	धनिन्
we/us two	आवाम्
went	अगच्छत् गतवत्
(they) were (pl.)	आसन्
(they two) were	आस्ताम्
(we) were (pl.)	आस्म
(we two) were	आस्व
(you) were (pl.)	आस्त
(you) were (pl.)	आसीः
(you two) were	आस्तम्
what?	किम्
whatever . . . that	
	यत् यत् . . . तत् तत्
wheel	अक्षः, चक्रम्
when?	कदा
when . . . then	यदा . . . तदा

where?	कुत्र
wheel formation	चक्रव्यूहः
Whirlwind demon, the	चक्रवातः
who? what?	कः, का, किम्
wife	भार्या
wind	वायुः
wine	मद्यम्
wing	पक्षः
(having) wisdom	धीमत्
wise	प्राज्ञ°, धीमत्
wise lady	ज्ञानिनी
wise man	ज्ञानिन्
wise teacher, priest	ब्राह्मणः
wish	वरः
with, together with	सह (+3rd)
womb	गर्भः
wood, forest	वनम्, अरण्यम्
word, command	वचनम्
world	लोकः
writes	लिखति

Y

Yaśodā	यशोदा
yellow	पीत°
you (singular)	त्वम्
you (plural)	यूयम्

you (plural, 2nd)	युष्मान्
you two (1st & 2nd)	युवाम्
(by) you (singular)	त्वया
(for) you (singular)	तुभ्यम्
(for) you (plural)	युष्मभ्यम्
(from) you (plural)	युष्मत्
(from) you (singular)	त्वत्
(in) you (singular)	त्वयि
(in/of) you two	युवयोः
(of) you (singular)	तव
your	तव
Yudhiṣṭhira	युधिष्ठिरः

APPENDIX 4

Vocabulary: Sanskrit – English

This Sanskrit–English vocabulary comprises in alphabetical order all Sanskrit words, with their appropriate English renderings, used in the exercises and stories found in Parts 1, 2 and 3 of this book, as well as those used in the earlier Sanskrit textbooks, 'The Stories of Krishna' and 'The Story of Rāma'.

अ

अकथयत्	told
अकरोत्	made, did, built
अकुर्वन्	they (pl.) made, did
अक्रियत	(it was) made, built
अक्रीडत्	(he/she) played
अक्रोशत्	cried out
अक्षः	wheel
अक्षिपत्	threw
अखादत्	ate
अखाद्यत	(was) eaten
अगच्छत्	went
अगायत्	sang
अग्निः	fire
अग्निमत्°	(having) fire
अघः	Agha, name of a demon
अङ्गुलः/अङ्गुली	thumb
अङ्गुलीयम्	ring
अचरत्	walked
अचलः	mountain

अचिन्तयत्	(he/she) thought
अचिरेण	soon
अजयत्	conquered
अतरत्	crossed
अतिष्ठत्	stood
अतीव	very
अतुदत्	hit
अतुद्यत	(was) hit
अत्र	here
अत्यजत्	(he/she) left, abandoned
अदग्ध°	unburnt
अददात्	gave
अदहत्	burned
अदाह्यत	set light to
अधः	beneath
अधर्मः	cheating, sin, unlawful act
अधावत्	ran
अधुना	now
अनन्त°	limitless
अनन्तरम्	straight away
अनमत्	bowed
अनयत्	led

अनाशयत्	destroyed	अमिलत् (+3rd)	met
अनुगच्छति	follows	अमृतम्	nectar of immortality
अनुधावति	runs after	अम्बालिका	Ambālikā
अनुधाव्य	(having) run after	अम्बा	Ambā
अनुभवति	experiences, feels	अम्बिका	Ambikā
अनुभूत॰	experienced	अयोध्या	Ayodhyā
अनेक॰	many	अरण्यम्	forest
अन्तः	inside; end	अरमत	rejoiced
अन्ते	in the end	अरिः	enemy
अन्ध॰	blind	अरुण॰	red
अन्नम्	food	अरोदत्	cried, wailed
अन्य॰	other, another	अर्जुनः	Arjuna
अन्वैच्छत्	searched after	-अर्थम्	for the sake of
अपगच्छति	goes away	अलभत	found
अपठत्	recited, read	अल्प॰	small
अपतत्	fell	अवगच्छति	goes down; understands
अपश्यत्	saw	अवदत्	said, spoke
अपहृत॰	carried off	अवरोहति	climbs down
अपि	also, even	अवर्धत	grew
(न कदा अपि	never)	अवसत्	dwelt
अपिबत्	drank	अशृणोत्	listened
अपीयत	was drunk	अशोकवृक्षाः	Aśoka trees
अपृच्छत्	asked	अश्वः	horse
अभय॰	fearless	अष्टम॰	eighth
अभवत्	became	असाधु॰	evil
अभितः	around	असि	you (sing.) are
अभिधावति	runs against, towards; attacks	अस्ति	is, exists
अभिषेकः	anointing; coronation	अस्थापयत्	placed, put
अभीत॰	fearless		

अन्वहृह्यत्	fell in love	आरोहति	climbs
अस्मत्	(from) us (plural)	आवयोः	(of/in) us two
अस्मभ्यम्	(for) us (plural)	आवाभ्याम्	(by/for/from) us two
अस्माकम्	(of) us (plural)	आवाम्	we/us two
अस्मान्	us (plural, 2nd)	आवृत॰	covered
अस्मासु	(in) us (plural)	आसन्	(they, plural) were
अस्मि	I am	आसम्	I was
अहम्	I	आसीः	you (sing.) were
अहसत्	laughed	आसीत्	he/she/it/there was
अहो	O my!	आस्त	you (plural) were
		आस्तम्	you two were
		आस्ताम्	they two were
		आस्म	we (plural) were
आ		आस्यम्	mouth
		आस्व	we two were
		आह	(he/she) said
आगच्छ	come! (sg.)		
आगच्छत्	came		
आगच्छत	come! (pl.)		
आगच्छति	comes		
आगच्छतु	(let) come	**इ**	
आगत॰	come		
आगतवत्॰	came		
आगमिष्यति	will come	इच्छति	he/she/it desires, wants
आगम्य	having come	इति	'thus'
आचार्यः	teacher	इदानीम्	now
आत्मनः (6th sg. of आत्मन्) his own, her own		इन्द्रः	Indra
		इन्द्रजित्	Indrajit
आनन्दः	bliss	इव	like, as if
आनय	bring!	इष्ट्वा	(having) desired, wanted
आनयत्	brought		
आनयति	brings		

189

ई	
ईर्ष्या	jealousy

उ	
उक्त°, उक्तवत्	said, spoken to
उत्तम°	best
उत्तरा	Uttarā
उत्तिष्ठति	stands up
उत्सवः	party
उदरः	belly
उदहरत्	lifted, lifted up
उदित्वा	having said
उद्भवति	arises
उद्भूय	having arisen
उद्यानम्	garden
उद्धरति	lifts, lifts up
उन्मिषति	opens eyes
उप–	towards, near
उपगच्छति	approaches
उपरम	stop!
उपरमति (+5th)	stops
उपविशति	sits down
उपहरति	bring near, place before
ऊरूः (m.)	thigh

उषित्वा	having lived, dwelt

ऋ	
ऋषिः (m.)	sage
ऋषभः	bull

ए	
एक° [*goes like* तत्]	one, a certain
एकदा	once, once upon a time
एकलव्यः	Ekalavya
एव	alone, only (emphasises previous word)
एवम्	thus; likewise
एषः, एषा, एतत्	this

ओ	
ओषधिः (f.)	plant

ऐ		का चन/अपि/चित्	someone, something, a certain
ऐच्छन्	(they) desired, wanted	कामः	desire
		कालः	time
औ		कालियः	Kāliya, a serpent demon
		कालेन	in time
औपनिषद॰	following the Upaniṣads	किम्	what?
		किम् चन/अपि/चित्	someone, something, a certain
क		कुक्कुरः	dog
		कुत्र	where?
कः	who? what?	कुन्ती	Kuntī
कः चित् (m.)	someone; a certain	कुपित॰	angry
कंसः	Kaṃsa	कुबेरः	Kubera, god of wealth
कण्ठः	throat	करोतु	(let) do
कन्या	daughter, girl	कुशल॰	skilled, able
कपिः (m.)	monkey	कृत॰, कृतवत्॰	done, made
कपोतः	pigeon	कृत्वा	having done, having made, having put on
करोति	does, makes, puts on	कृष्ण॰	black
कर्णः	ear; Karṇa	कृष्णः	Kṛṣṇa
कर्मन् (n.)	action	केशः	hair
का	who? what?	कैकेयी	Kaikeyī
काकः	crow	कौरवः	Kaurava
		कौसल्या	Kausalyā
		क्रीडति	plays
		क्रीडित्वा	having played
		क्रोशति	cries out

क्षणः	a moment	गच्छतु	let (him/her/it) go
क्षत्रियः	brave warrior or king	गजः	elephant
क्षिपति	throws, shoots	गत॰	gone
क्षिप्त॰	shot	गतवत्	went
क्षिप्त्वा	having thrown, shot	गत्वा	having gone
		गदा	a mace, club
		गन्धः	a smell

		गमिष्यति	will go
		गमिष्यते	will be gone to
		गर्दभः	donkey
		गर्भः	womb
खगः	bird	गर्वित॰	proud
खड्गः	sword	गान्धारी	Gāndhārī
खाद	eat! (singular)	गायति	sings
खादत	eat! (plural)	गुरुः	teacher
खादति	eats	गुहा	cave
खादित॰	eaten	गृध्रः	vulture
खादितवत्	ate	गृहम्	house
खादिष्यति	will eat	गृहीत॰	grabbed
खादिष्यते	will be eaten	गृहीत्वा	having grabbed
खाद्यते	is eaten	गोपालः	cowherd
		ग्रीवः	neck

गगनम्	sky		
गङ्गा	Gaṅgā (a goddess)		
गच्छ	go! (singular)	घोर॰	horrible
गच्छत	go! (plural)	घृध्रः	vulture
गच्छति	goes		

च

च	and
चक्रम्	wheel
चक्रवातः	the Whirlwind demon
चक्रव्यूहः	wheel formation
चन	(*indefinite after* कः, का *or* किम्)
चन्द्रः	moon
चर (sg.), चरत (pl.)	walk!
चरति	walks
चरित्वा	having walked
चरिष्यते	will be walked to
चाणूरः	Cāṇūra
चापः	bow
चित्	(*see* चन)
चिन्तयति	thinks
चिन्तयित्वा	having thought
चिन्तयिष्यते	will be thought of
चिबुकम्	chin
चिरेण	for a long time

छ

छित्त्वा	having cut
छिन्न॰	cut

ज

जटायुः	Jaṭāyu
जनः	person
जनाः	people
जनकः	father
जनकः	Janaka
जननी	mother
जयति	is victorious, conquers
जयतु	let be victorious
जलम्	water
जलाशयः	lake
जात॰	born
जितः	conquered
जीव (sg.), जीवत (pl.)	live!
जीवति	lives
जीवित्वा	having lived
जुहोति	sacrifices
जेष्यति	will conquer
ज्ञात॰	known
ज्ञानिन्	a wise man
ज्ञानिनी	a wise lady
ज्येष्ठ॰	eldest

त

तत्	that / it
ततः	after that, therefore, hence

तत्र	there	तृणम्	grass
तदा	then	ते	those (m. pl.)
तपस् (n.)	fire, discipline, austerity	तेन	by him / by that
तम्	that, him (2nd)	तौ (m.)	those two
तमस् (n.)	darkness	त्यक्त॰	abandoned
तयोः	(of/in) those two	त्यक्त्वा	having left
तरति	crosses	त्यज	leave alone! (sg.)
तर्हि	then, at that time	त्यजत	leave alone! (pl.)
तव	your, of you	त्यजति	leaves
तस्मात्	therefore	त्रि	three
तस्मिन्	in that, in him	त्वत्	from you (sg.)
तस्मिन् एव काले/क्षणे	at that very time/moment	त्वम्	you (sg.)
		त्वया	by you (sg.)
तस्मै	to that, to him	त्वयि	in you (sg.)
तस्य	his, of him		
तस्याः	her, of her		
तस्यै	to her	**द**	
ताटका	Tāṭakā		
तान्	those (2nd pl. m.)	दग्ध॰	burnt
ताम्	her (2nd)	दग्ध्वा	having burnt, having set alight
तारका	star	दण्डय	punish!
तिरोहित॰	hidden	दत्त॰	given
तिष्ठति	stands	दत्त्वा	having given
त्रि–	three	ददाति	gives
तीरम्	bank (of a river)	दयया	please
तु	but	दशरथः	Daśaratha
तुदति	hits	दष्ट॰	bitten
तुभ्यम्	for you (4th sg.)	दहति	burns
तूष्णीम्	silent		

194

दह्यते	is burnt
दानम्	gift
दास्यति	will give
दाहयति	sets light to
दीर्घ॰	long
दुर्गन्धः	bad smell
दर्जनः	bad person
दुर्मङ्गलम्	bad omen
दुर्योधनः	Duryodhana
दुष्कृत॰	ill done, evil
दुष्ट॰	evil
दुःखम्	unhappiness, sorrow
दुःखित॰	sad
दुःखेन	unhappily
दुःशासनः	Duhśāsana
दूतः	messenger
दूरम्	a long way
दूरे	far away
दृष्ट॰	seen
दृष्टवत्	saw
दृष्ट्वा	having seen
देवः	a god
देवी	goddess
देहः	body
देहि	give! (sing.)
दोषः	fault
द्रक्ष्यति	will see
द्रोणः	Drona
द्वारम्	door

द्वितीय॰	second
द्रक्ष्यति	will see
द्रक्ष्यते	it will be seen

ध

धक्ष्यति	will burn
धनिन्॰	having wealth; virtuous
धर्मः	law, righteousness, justice
धार्मिक॰	righteous, just
धातृ (m.)	creator
धाव (sg.), धावत (pl.)	run!
धावति	runs
धावतु	let run
धावितवत्॰	ran
धीमत्॰	having wisdom, wise
धीवरः	fisherman
धृतराष्ट्रः	Dhṛtarāṣṭra

न

न	not
न कदा अपि	never
न किञ्चित्	nothing
न कुत्र चित्	nowhere

नकुलः	Nakula
नगरम्	town, city
नग्न॰	naked
नत्वा	having bowed
नदी	river
नमति	bows
नमस् (n.)	bow, homage
नयति	leads
नरः	man
नलः	Nala
नव॰	new
नवनीतम्	butter
नष्ट॰	ruined, destroyed
नागः	magical snake
नाटकः	dancer
नाम	a name; by name
नामन् (n.)	name
नारङ्ग॰	orange
नारदः	Nārada, a sage
नारी	lady
नाशयति	destroys
नासिका	nose
निक्षिपति	throws down;
	places trust in
निमग्न॰	sunk
निमिषति	closes the eyes
निमिष्य	having closed the eyes
निर्गच्छति	goes out
निवसति	lives in, inhabits

निषादः	outcast
नीत्वा	having led
नील॰	blue
नीलः	Nīla (a monkey architect)
नृपः	king
नेत्रम्	eye
नेष्यति	will lead
नौका	boat

प

पङ्कः	mud
पक्षः	wing
पक्षिन्, पक्षिनी	bird
पञ्च॰	five
पठति	reads, recites
पतति	falls
पतिः	husband, lord
पतितवत्	fell
पतित्वा	having fallen
पत्नी	wife
परमेश्वरः	the Supreme Lord
परिणयति	marries
परिणीय	having married
परीक्षा	test
पर्णगृहम्	leaf-house

पर्यष्वजत	embraced
पशवः (pl of पशु)	cattle
पश्य	see! (singular)
पश्यत	see! (plural)
पश्यति	sees
पश्यतु	let see
पाण्डवः	Pāṇḍava
पाण्डु॰	pale
पाण्डुः	Pāṇḍu
पादः	foot
पितामहः	the Creator
पिब	drink! (singular)
पिबत	drink! (plural)
पिबति	drinks
पीठम्	chair
पीडित॰	tormented
पीत॰	yellow; drunk
पीयते	is drunk
पुच्छम्, पुच्छः	tail
पुत्रः	son
पुनः	again
पुनः पुनः	again and again
पुरा	long ago
पुरुषः	person
पुष्पम्	flower
पुस्तकम्	book
पूतना	Pūtanā, a demoness
पूर्ण॰	filled
पूर्वम्	previously

पृच्छति	asks
पृष्ट्वा	having asked
प्रगच्छति	goes forward
प्रति (+ 2nd)	towards
प्रतिगच्छति	goes back, returns
प्रतिवदति	replies, answers
प्रत्यागच्छति	comes back
प्रत्युद्य	having replied
प्रथम॰	first
प्रपुत्रः	grandson
प्रबल॰	strong
प्रविशति	enters
प्रविश्य	having entered
प्रहसति	bursts into laughter, laughs aloud
प्राज्ञ॰	wise
प्रातराशः	breakfast
प्रार्थयति	asks for
प्राविशत्	entered
प्रिय॰	dear
प्लवनम्	a jump

फ

फलम्	fruit

ब		भवति	becomes
		भवतु	let become
		भविष्यति	will become
बद्ध्वा	having bound	भागः	part
बध्नाति	binds	भाति	shines
बलवत्॰	having strength	भार्या	wife
बलिष्ठ॰	mighty, strongest	भिन्न॰	broken
बहु॰	many, much	भीत॰	afraid, frightened
बहुकालम्	for a long time	भीमः	Bhīma
बालकः	boy	भीष्मः	Bhīṣma
बाहुः (m.)	arm	भूतवत्	became
बिडालः	cat	भूत्वा	having become
बुद्ध॰	awake	भूमिम् (2nd)	ground, earth
बुद्धिः (f.)	intellect, intelligence	भूमिः (f.)	ground, earth
ब्रह्मास्त्रम्	the Brahmā weapon	भूम्याम्	on the ground
		भूषणम्	jewel
ब्राह्मणः	a wise teacher or priest	भेदयति	splits, breaks, destroys
		भ्रातृ	brother
भ			
		म	
भगवत्॰	having good fortune; blessed; lord		
भयम्	fear	मणिः	jewel
भरतः	Bharata	मण्डलम्	ball
भर्तृ (m.)	husband	मत्	from me
भव	be!, become! (sg.)	मतिः (f.)	thought
भवत	be!, become! (pl.)	मत्स्यः	fish

मध्ये (+6th)	in the middle of	मृगः	deer, forest animal
मनस् (n.)	mind	मृत॰	dead
मनुष्यः	man	मेघः	cloud
मन्त्रः	mantra		
मन्त्रिन् (m.)	counsellor, minister		

य

मम	my, of me	यत् यत्....तत् तत्	whatever...that
मया	by me	यतः	since
मयि	in me	यथा...तथा	as . . . so
मरणम्	death	यदा...तदा	when . . . then
महत्॰	great	यदि	if
महा-	great-	यशोदा	Yaśodā
मह्यम्	for me	यस्मात्...तस्मात्	since . . . therefore
मातृ (f.)	mother	यावत्....तावत्	as long as . . . so long
माद्री	Mādrī	युक्त॰ (+ 3rd)	possessing
माम्	me (2nd)	युद्धम्	battle
माया	magic	युद्धम् करोति	does battle
मारीचः	Mārīca	युधिष्ठिरः	Yudhiṣṭhira
मार्गः	road	युवयोः	of / in you two
मित्रम्	friend	युवराजः	heir apparent
मिथिला	Mithilā (a city)	युवाभ्याम्	by / for / from you two
मिलति (+ 3rd)	meets	युवाम्	you two (1st or 2nd)
मिलित्वा	having met		
मुक्त॰ (+ 5th)	freed	युष्मत्	from you (pl.)
मुखम्	mouth, face	युष्मभ्यम्	for you (pl.)
मुनिः	sage	युष्माकम्	of you (pl.)
मुनिजनः	monk, sage	युष्मान्	you (2nd pl.)
मूढवत्	like a fool		
मूर्तिः (f.)	body, statue		

युष्माभिः	by you (pl.)
युष्मासु	in you (pl.)
यूयम्	you (1st pl.)

र

रक्तम्	blood
रक्ष	protect!
रक्षति	saves, protects
रक्षित॰	saved, protected
रक्षित्वा	having saved
रजस् (n.)	dust, dirt, impurity
रथः	chariot
रमणीय॰	beautiful
रमते	rejoices
राक्षसः	demon
राक्षसी	demoness
राजगृहम्	palace
राजन् (m.)	king
राजपुत्रः	prince
राज्यम्	kingdom
राज्ञी	queen
रात्रिः (f.)	night
रामः	Rāma
रामवत्	like Rāma
रावणः	Rāvaṇa, king of the demons
राहुः	Rāhu (a demon)

रुचिर॰	beautiful
रूपम्	form
रूपवत्॰	having a beautiful form; handsome
रोदति	cries; wails

ल

लक्ष्मणः	Lakṣmaṇa
लङ्का	Laṅkā, Rāvaṇa's island
लप्स्यते	will find
लब्ध॰	found
लब्ध्वा	having found
लभते	finds
ललाटम्	forehead
लिखति	writes
लोकः	world

व

वचनम्	word; command, statement
वत्सः	calf
वद (sg.)／ ॰त (pl.)	speak!
वदति	speaks, says
वदतु	let speak
वदिष्यति	will speak

वनम्	forest	विस्मित॰	amazed
वन्दनम्	thank you	वीर॰	brave
वयम्	we (plural)	वीरः	warrior, hero
वरः	wish	वृक्षः	tree
वर्णः	colour	वृत॰	chosen
वर्धते	grows	वृद्ध॰	old
वर्धिष्यते	will grow	वैश्यः	trader, producer, farmer
वर्षाः	rains		
वंशः	flute	व्याघ्रः	tiger
वसति	dwells	व्याधः	hunter
वस्त्रम्	garment	व्यापादयति	kills
वादयति	plays (an instrument)	व्यापादय	kill!
		व्यापादयिष्यति	will kill
वानरः	monkey	व्यापादित॰	killed
वायुः	wind	व्यापादितवत्॰	killed
वायुपुत्रः	Hanumān, son of the wind	व्यासः	Vyāsa
		व्रतम्	vow
विवरः	an opening, hole		
विवाहः	marriage		
विचित्रवीर्यः	Vicitravīrya	**श**	
विषम्	poison		
विशाल॰	large	शतम्	hundred (+6th pl.)
विशिष्ट॰	special	शत्रुः	enemy
विश्वामित्रः	Viśvāmitra	शत्रुघ्नः	Śatrughna
विसर्गः	a release of the breath, shown by ः, as in रामः	शप्त॰	cursed
		शब्दः	sound, voice
		शरः	arrow
विस्मयः	astonishment, amazement	शशकः	rabbit
विस्मरति	forgets	शान्तनुः	Śāntanu

शान्तिः (f.)	peace		
शापः	curse		
शाला	room, hall		
शिरस् (n.)	head		
शिला	rock		
शिवः	Śiva		
शिष्यः	pupil		
शीघ्रम्	quickly		
शुद्ध॰	pure		
शूद्रः	servant, labourer		
शूर्पणखा	Śūrpaṇakhā		
शृणु	listen! (singular)		
शृणुत	listen! (plural)		
शृणोति	hears, listens		
शृणोतु	let listen		
शोकः	grief		
श्रान्त॰	exhausted		
श्री (f)	light		
श्रुत॰	(was) heard		
श्रुतवत्	heard		
श्रुत्वा	having heard		
श्रेष्ठ॰	best		

ष

षष्॰	six
षष्ठ॰	sixth

म

सत्य॰	true
सत्यवती	Satyavatī
सन्ति	they (plural) are
संतुष्ट॰	contented
संधिः (f.)	(*in grammar*) meeting of sounds
सप्त	seven
समागच्छति	come together, gather
समाप्त॰	finished
समीपे (+ 6th)	near
समुद्रः	ocean
सर्पः	snake
सर्व॰	all
सर्वत्र	everywhere
सर्वम्	all, everything
सस्मितम्	with a smile
सह (+ 3rd)	together with
सहदेवः	Sahadeva
सः	he / that
सा	she / that
साधु॰	good
साधु साधु	good! good!
साहाय्यम्	help

साहाय्यम् करिष्यति	will give help
सिंहः	lion
सीता	Sītā
सुखम्	happiness, pleasure
सुखित॰	happy
सुगन्धः	good smell
सुग्रीवः	Sugrīva
सुन्दर॰, -री॰(f.)	handsome; beautiful
सुमित्रा	Sumitrā
सुवर्ण॰	golden
सुहृद् (m.)	friend
सूतः	charioteer
सूत्रम्	rope, string; rule, aphorism; thread
सूर्यः	sun
सेतुः	causeway
सेना	army
सेवकः	servant, attendant
सोदरः	brother
सैनिकः	soldier
स्तनः	breast
स्तम्भः	pillar
स्तः	they two are
स्थ	you (pl.) are
स्थः	you two are
स्थापयति	places
स्निग्ध्वा	having been fond of
स्निह्यति (+7th)	falls in love
स्म	(gives past tense to present verb)
स्मः	we (pl.) are
स्वदेहः	own body
स्वप्नः	dream, sleep
स्वयंवरः	self-choice ceremony
स्वरः	voice; vowel
स्वर्गः	heaven
स्वः	we two are
स्वसृ (f.)	sister
स्वामिन् (m.)	master

ह

हत॰	killed
हत्वा	having killed
हरित॰	green
हरिः	the Lord
हसति	laughs
हसित्वा	having laughed
हस्तः	hand
हा हा	alas! alas!
हृदयम्	heart
हे	O!
ह्रस्व॰	short

Seven Sanskrit Coursebooks for Beginners

The first group of books entitled **Sanskrit is Fun** (Parts I-III) introduce the learners to the *Devanagari* alphabets, grouping the letters according to their place of articulation, called 'Family', which comprises both the vowels and consonants.

Learners are first taught how to draw the letters. Learning and teaching is also helped by the humorous presentation of the letters in the form of animals figures. The next step is to add vowel to the consonants, and then to teach joint (compound) consonants. Finally words and sentences are formed.

Pages: viii, 76

Pages: viii, 76

Pages: viii, 60

ISBN: 978-81-208-3545-0 Pt. I (Paper)
ISBN: 978-81-208-3590-0 (Spiral Bound)
ISBN: 978-81-208-3546-7 Pt. II (Paper)
ISBN: 978-81-208-3591-7 (Spiral Bound)

ISBN: 978-81-208-3547-4 Pt. III (Paper)
ISBN: 978-81-208-3592-4 (Spiral Bound)
ISBN: 978-81-208-3597-9 (3 Pts. Cloth Set)

Pages: xiv, 162

Pages: xv, 189

The second group of books seek to teach Sanskrit with reference to the age-old stories of Krishna and Rama. **The Stories of Krishna** (Parts I-II) cover full declensions of the most common type of masculine, feminine and neuter nouns: conjugations of a simple verb in the present, future and past tenses and twelve stories based on the childhood of Krishna.

ISBN: 978-81-208-3548-1 Pt. I (Paper)
ISBN: 978-81-208-3593-1 (Spiral Bound)
ISBN: 978-81-208-3549-8 Pt. II (Paper)
ISBN: 978-81-208-3594-8 (Spiral Bound)
ISBN: 978-81-208-3598-6 (2 Pts. Cloth Set)

The Story of Rama books (Parts I – II) together relate, in 16 episodes, the story of the Ramayana. Part I introduces : the standard method of transliteration; the gerund ('having done something'); and the declension of the Sanskrit word for 'that' in all three genders. Part II covers an introduction to the imperative mood; other important noun and pronoun declensions; 'having done something' used with prefixes; the past passive participle; the conjugation of the middle voice and the verb 'to be' in present, future and past tenses; and the completion of the standard method of transliteration.

Pages: xviii, 125

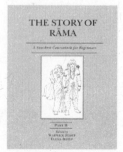

Pages: xiv, 137

ISBN: 978-81-208-3550-4 Pt. I (Paper)
ISBN: 978-81-208-3595-5 (Spiral Bound)
ISBN: 978-81-208-3551-1 Pt. II (Paper)

ISBN: 978-81-208-3596-2 (Spiral Bound)
ISBN: 978-81-208-3599-3 (2 Pts. Cloth Set)